INTRODUCTION TO ANDROID DEVELOPMENT WITH KOTLIN

Developing Android apps using Kotlin, including UI design and handling system resources

NATHAN WESTWOOD

TABLE OF CONTENTS

ABOUT THE AUTHOR!

Dr. Nathan Westwood

Biography:

Dr. Nathan Westwood is a pioneering technologist known for his exceptional contributions to the fields of software development, cloud computing, and artificial intelligence. With a passion for innovation and a relentless drive to solve complex problems, Nathan has become a prominent figure in the tech industry, shaping the future of digital technology.

Born and raised in Silicon Valley, Nathan's interest in technology started at a young age. His fascination with computers and coding led him to pursue a degree in Computer Science from Stanford University, where he excelled academically and honed his skills in programming and software engineering. During his time at Stanford, Nathan was involved in several cutting-edge projects that sparked his interest in AI and cloud technologies.

After graduating, Nathan joined a leading tech firm where he played a key role in developing cloud-based solutions that revolutionized data storage and analytics. His work in the early stages of cloud computing set the foundation for modern infrastructure-as-a-service (IaaS) platforms, earning him recognition as one of the industry's emerging stars. As a lead engineer, Nathan was instrumental in launching products that have since become industry standards.

Nathan's entrepreneurial spirit led him to co-found his own tech startup focused on AI-driven automation tools for businesses. Under his leadership, the company rapidly gained traction, attracting both investors and clients who were eager to leverage his innovative AI solutions to streamline operations and improve efficiency. Nathan's commitment to pushing the boundaries of what's possible in tech quickly earned him a reputation as a visionary leader.

Known for his expertise in machine learning, Nathan has also worked with several large tech companies, advising on the integration of AI and data science into their operations. His work has spanned various sectors, including healthcare, finance, and manufacturing, where he has helped organizations harness the power of data and automation to achieve exponential growth.

Beyond his technical achievements, Nathan is a sought-after speaker at global tech conferences, where he shares his insights on the future of cloud computing, artificial intelligence, and the ethical challenges posed by emerging technologies. His thought leadership and commitment to ethical innovation have made him a respected voice in the tech community.

In addition to his professional accomplishments, Nathan is deeply passionate about mentoring the next generation of tech leaders. He regularly contributes to educational programs and initiatives designed to inspire young minds and equip them with the skills necessary to thrive in the ever-evolving tech landscape.

Nathan Westwood continues to be a trailblazer in the tech industry, shaping the future of technology with his innovative ideas, entrepreneurial spirit, and commitment to making a positive impact on the world.

CHAPTER 1: GETTING STARTED WITH KOTLIN

1. Introduction to Kotlin: The Why and How of Kotlin as the Primary Language for Android

1.1 The Evolution of Android Development:

The landscape of Android development has been evolving since its inception. Initially dominated by Java, Android development saw the emergence of Kotlin in 2017, when it was officially announced as a first-class language for Android by Google. But why Kotlin? Java was, and still is, a robust and reliable language, but Kotlin was designed to address several pain points that developers faced with Java, such as verbosity, null pointer exceptions, and slow compilation speeds.

Kotlin is a modern, statically typed programming language built to be fully interoperable with Java. It's concise, expressive, and designed with modern features like null safety, extension functions, and higher-order functions, making it a great choice for Android development. With Google's full support for Kotlin, it's become the de facto language for Android app development.

1.2 Why Kotlin? A Developer's Perspective:

Kotlin was designed to be a better alternative to Java without replacing it entirely. While Java is still widely used, Kotlin enhances productivity by offering the following advantages:

- **Concise Syntax:** Kotlin allows developers to write less code to achieve the same functionality. This is achieved through features such as data classes, lambda expressions, and more concise syntax for standard operations.

- **Null Safety:** One of the main challenges with Java was handling null references. Kotlin introduces null safety with the ? operator to prevent NullPointerException errors, which are one of the most common runtime exceptions in Java.

- **Interoperability with Java:** Kotlin is fully interoperable with Java, allowing developers to use Java libraries, frameworks, and tools while writing Kotlin code. This enables a smooth transition for teams already using Java without rewriting their entire codebase.

- **Coroutines for Asynchronous Programming:** Kotlin provides built-in support for asynchronous programming with coroutines. This allows developers to write non-blocking code that is simple and easy to read, unlike Java's thread-based concurrency.

- **Tooling Support:** Kotlin works seamlessly with Android Studio, offering excellent support for development tools like code completion, refactoring, debugging, and more.

By the end of this section, you will understand why Kotlin is quickly becoming the go-to language for Android development and why it is crucial for modern Android developers to master it.

1.3 Kotlin Features in a Nutshell:

Kotlin has several standout features that enhance productivity and code quality, making it a popular choice among Android developers:

- **Null Safety:** By introducing nullable and non-nullable types, Kotlin helps avoid one of the most dreaded bugs in Java development — the infamous NullPointerException. In Kotlin, if a variable can be null, it is explicitly declared as nullable (Type?), ensuring the developer handles it properly.

- **Extension Functions:** Kotlin allows you to extend the functionality of existing classes without modifying them. This feature is particularly helpful when working with Android SDK classes, enabling the addition of utility methods.

- **Smart Casts:** Kotlin's type system performs automatic casting when it's safe to do so. For example, if you check a variable's type, Kotlin automatically casts it to the required type, reducing the need for manual casting and making the code cleaner and more readable.

- **Data Classes:** Kotlin has a special type of class known as a data class. This class automatically generates equals(), hashCode(), toString(), and other utility functions, reducing boilerplate code when working with objects that hold data.

- **Coroutines:** Kotlin's support for coroutines simplifies asynchronous programming. Instead of dealing with complex callback chains or thread management, developers can write asynchronous code that is as simple as synchronous code.

2. Setting Up Your Development Environment

2.1 Installing Android Studio:

To start developing Android apps with Kotlin, you'll need to set up your development environment, which includes installing **Android Studio**. Android Studio is the official integrated development environment (IDE) for Android development, and it comes with all the necessary tools to write, test, and deploy Android apps.

Here's how to set up Android Studio:

1. **Download Android Studio:**

   o   Visit the official Android developer website and download the latest stable version of Android Studio for your operating system (Windows, macOS, or Linux).

2. **Install Android Studio:**

   o   Follow the installation instructions for your operating system. On Windows, this typically involves running the installer, while macOS users can drag the Android Studio app to their Applications folder.

3. **Start Android Studio:**

   o   Once the installation is complete, open Android Studio. The first time you launch Android Studio, it will ask you to set up a few initial preferences. Select the default settings unless you have specific preferences.

4. **Install SDK and Virtual Devices:**

- Android Studio will prompt you to install the Android SDK (Software Development Kit) and configure a virtual device (emulator) for testing apps. Follow the prompts to install these components.

5. **Set Up Kotlin:**

   - Kotlin support comes bundled with Android Studio starting from version 3.0, but if for some reason you need to install or enable Kotlin manually, you can do so by navigating to Preferences > Plugins and searching for Kotlin. If it's not installed, simply click **Install**.

2.2 Configuring Android Studio for Kotlin:

Once you have Android Studio up and running, you'll need to configure it to support Kotlin development. Fortunately, this step is straightforward.

1. **Enable Kotlin in a New Project:**

   - When you create a new Android project in Android Studio, you'll be prompted to choose the programming language for your app. Select **Kotlin** from the language options.

2. **Enable Kotlin for an Existing Project:**

   - If you're working on an existing Java-based Android project, adding Kotlin is simple. Open the build.gradle file (Project level) and ensure that Kotlin is included in the dependencies block:

gradle

classpath "org.jetbrains.kotlin:kotlin-gradle-plugin:1.5.0"

- o Sync the project with Gradle files, and Android Studio will automatically configure the project to support Kotlin.

3. **Testing Your Environment:**

- o Create a simple Kotlin file in your project to test if everything is set up correctly. If the code runs without any issues, your environment is ready for development.

2.3 Understanding the Android Studio Interface:

Android Studio's interface is rich with features that make it easier to develop Android apps. Key sections of the IDE include:

- **Editor Window:** This is where you'll write your code. Android Studio provides syntax highlighting, code completion, and error detection to help streamline the coding process.

- **Project View:** This panel shows the file structure of your Android project, including the src/ folder where your Kotlin files are located.

- **Toolbars and Navigation:** These include tools for building, running, and debugging your app, as well as access to the terminal, Git version control, and settings.

By now, you should be comfortable with Android Studio and ready to start coding in Kotlin.

3. Your First Kotlin Program: A Hands-on Example of a Simple Kotlin Console Application

3.1 Writing the First Kotlin Program:

Now that you have Kotlin set up in Android Studio, let's dive into writing a simple Kotlin program. This is a console-based program that takes user input and outputs a greeting.

1. **Create a New Kotlin File:**

    o   In Android Studio, go to the src folder of your project, right-click, and select **New > Kotlin File/Class.** Name it Main.

2. **Write Your First Kotlin Code:** In the new file, type the following code:

kotlin

```
fun main() {
    println("Enter your name:")
    val name = readLine()
    println("Hello, $name! Welcome to Kotlin.")
}
```
Let's break this code down:

    o   fun main(): This is the entry point of any Kotlin application. Just like in Java, the main() function is the starting point.

    o   println(): This function prints a message to the console.

    o   readLine(): This reads user input from the console and stores it in the name variable.

- val: This keyword declares a read-only variable, meaning it cannot be reassigned once initialized.

3. **Run Your Program:**

   - In Android Studio, click the **Run** button or use the shortcut Shift + F10. The console window will appear, asking for user input. Enter your name, and the program will greet you back.

3.2 Understanding the Code:

This simple example introduces you to basic Kotlin syntax:

- **Functions**: fun main() defines the main function, which is the entry point of the program.

- **Variables**: val is used to declare a variable, and readLine() is used to capture user input.

- **String Interpolation**: The $name syntax is an example of Kotlin's string interpolation, which is a cleaner alternative to string concatenation.

3.3 Moving Forward:

This first program introduces you to Kotlin's syntax and helps you get comfortable with basic concepts. As you move forward, you'll build more complex Android applications using the same principles, but with added functionality such as creating user interfaces, handling data, and integrating APIs.

Conclusion

By now, you should have a solid understanding of why Kotlin is the go-to language for Android development, how to set up your development environment, and how to write your first Kotlin program. In the next sections, we'll delve deeper into building Android apps using Kotlin, focusing on Android-specific components and exploring real-world applications.

CHAPTER 2: UNDERSTANDING THE ANDROID STUDIO ENVIRONMENT

2.1 Navigating Android Studio: Overview of the IDE, Key Features, and Tools

Android Studio is the official Integrated Development Environment (IDE) for Android development. It's built on IntelliJ IDEA, a popular Java-based IDE, and tailored specifically to Android development. With Android Studio, developers can write code, design interfaces, test apps, and deploy them all in one place. The IDE comes packed with tools and features that optimize the development workflow and enhance productivity. In this section, we'll take a deep dive into Android Studio, focusing on key features and how to navigate the IDE.

The Layout of Android Studio

When you first launch Android Studio, you'll encounter a clean, well-organized interface that is designed for maximum efficiency. Here's a breakdown of the main components of the Android Studio interface:

- **Toolbars and Navigation Bar:** Located at the top of the window, these provide quick access to essential tools like running the app, debugging, version control, and file navigation.

- **Run Button:** The green arrow is used to run the app on an emulator or device.

- **Debug Button:** The bug icon is used for running your app in debug mode.

- **Gradle Sync:** The Gradle sync button is essential for syncing your project dependencies and configuration files with the Gradle build system.

- **Project Tool Window:** Located on the left, this window displays the structure of your Android project. You can toggle between various views (e.g., Android, Project, and Packages). This window provides an overview of all the resources, source code, and libraries in your project.

  - **Project View:** This default view shows the file structure with directories like src, res, build.gradle, etc.

  - **Android View:** This view is specialized for Android projects, displaying resources like layout files, drawable assets, and values in a structured manner.

- **Editor Window:** The editor window is the heart of Android Studio. It's where you'll write and edit your code. The editor supports multiple file types such as Kotlin, XML, and Gradle scripts. It also provides intelligent code completion, syntax highlighting, and real-time error checking to ensure your code is correct.

- **Toolbar for Gradle and Version Control:** The toolbar located just above the editor includes shortcuts for tasks related to version control (e.g., Git) and Gradle tasks such as building and running your project.

- **Logcat Window:** The Logcat window at the bottom displays logs from your app while it's running. This is crucial for debugging, as it provides real-time output for messages, errors, and exceptions generated by your app.

Key Features of Android Studio

1. **Code Completion and Smart Suggestions:** Android Studio offers intelligent code completion, which significantly speeds up your development process. As you type, the IDE will suggest method names, variable names, and even complete code snippets based on your context.

2. **Refactoring Tools:** Refactoring is essential for maintaining clean, readable, and reusable code. Android Studio provides various refactoring tools that can automatically rename variables, change method signatures, and even restructure your code without breaking the app.

3. **Linting and Error Checking:** Android Studio has built-in linting tools that automatically check for potential errors and warnings in your code. It highlights problematic areas in your code in real-time and provides quick fixes or suggestions for resolving these issues.

4. **Integrated Emulator and Device Management:** The Android Emulator is one of the key features that distinguishes Android Studio from other IDEs. It allows you to run your Android apps on a virtual device without needing a physical Android device. This emulator can simulate various device configurations, screen sizes, and OS versions.

5. **Version Control Integration:** Android Studio has integrated Git and other version control systems (VCS). You can commit changes, view diffs, resolve conflicts, and push

changes all from within the IDE, making collaboration much easier.

6. **Gradle Integration:** Gradle is a powerful build automation tool used in Android Studio to manage dependencies and build configurations. Android Studio integrates Gradle seamlessly, allowing you to automate the building and deployment process, handle multi-module projects, and work with third-party libraries.

7. **UI Design with Layout Editor:** Android Studio features a visual layout editor that lets you design user interfaces without having to manually write XML code. You can drag and drop UI elements like buttons, text fields, and images onto a virtual screen to build a responsive interface. The layout editor supports both design-time previews and live preview updates when changes are made.

8. **Profiler and Debugging Tools:** The Profiler tool allows you to monitor your app's performance, including memory usage, CPU usage, and network activity. Combined with debugging tools like breakpoints and step-through execution, Android Studio is designed to give you complete visibility into your app's performance.

9. **Testing and Unit Testing:** Android Studio provides integrated testing tools that allow you to run unit tests, UI tests, and instrumented tests. It also offers easy integration with frameworks like JUnit and Espresso for automated testing.

Navigating Android Studio Efficiently

Learning to navigate Android Studio effectively is crucial for speeding up your development process. Here are a few tips to help you get the most out of the IDE:

- **Use Keyboard Shortcuts:** Android Studio is full of keyboard shortcuts that save time. For example, Ctrl + Space triggers code completion, Ctrl + Shift + A brings up the "Find Action" dialog, and Shift + F10 runs the app.

- **Split the Editor:** You can split the editor window into multiple panes to view different files at the same time. This is particularly useful when working with both Kotlin code and XML layout files simultaneously.

- **Use the Navigation Bar:** Located just below the main toolbar, the navigation bar allows you to jump quickly between different files and folders in your project without navigating the file tree.

2.2 Creating Your First Android Project: Understanding Project Structure and Key Files

Now that you're familiar with Android Studio's interface, let's move on to creating your first Android project. Understanding the structure of an Android project is essential for managing your app's resources and source code effectively.

Creating a New Android Project

To create a new project in Android Studio, follow these steps:

1. **Open Android Studio and Start a New Project:**

   o Once you launch Android Studio, click on **Start a New Android Studio Project**. Android Studio will prompt you to enter a project name, package name, and save location. Choose the appropriate configurations for your app (e.g., language Kotlin, API level).

2. **Choosing the Template:**

   o Android Studio offers several project templates, including **Empty Activity**, **Basic Activity**, and **Navigation Drawer Activity**. For our first app, select the **Empty Activity** template, as it provides a blank slate to start your development.

3. **Configuring Your Project:**

   o In the next screen, you'll set the details of your project. Choose Kotlin as the programming language and select the minimum SDK (Android version) your app will support. For a simple app, the default API level (usually API 21, Lollipop) is fine.

4. **Project Creation:**

   o After hitting **Finish**, Android Studio will generate the necessary project files and directories. The IDE will sync the project with Gradle, download dependencies, and index the project files.

Understanding Project Structure

The default Android project structure is organized to help you manage your app's resources and source code efficiently. Here's a breakdown of the key files and directories:

- **app/src/main/java/**: This directory contains the source code of your app. By default, it includes a package with a MainActivity Kotlin file (the entry point of your app).

- **app/src/main/res/**: This is where all your resources, such as images, layout files, strings, and styles, are stored. It's divided into subdirectories like:

  - **layout/**: Contains XML files that define the app's user interfaces.

  - **drawable/**: Contains image files used in the app.

  - **values/**: Contains XML files defining constants like strings, colors, and dimensions.

- **app/src/main/AndroidManifest.xml**: This file is essential for Android apps. It declares the app's components (activities, services, etc.) and its permissions (e.g., internet access or location services).

- **build.gradle (Project and App Level):** Gradle is an automated build system used in Android Studio to manage dependencies, build configurations, and more. The build.gradle files at the project and app levels help configure the app's build process.

2.3 Running Your App on an Emulator: Setting Up an Android Emulator and Running Your First App

One of the greatest features of Android Studio is its ability to run your app on an emulator. The emulator simulates an Android device on your computer, allowing you to test your app without needing a physical device.

Setting Up an Android Emulator

Follow these steps to set up and configure an Android Emulator:

1. **Open AVD Manager:**

   o In Android Studio, click on the **AVD Manager** (Android Virtual Device) icon in the toolbar. This will open a window where you can create and manage virtual devices.

2. **Create a New Virtual Device:**

   o Click **Create Virtual Device** and choose a hardware profile. You can choose from a variety of devices, such as Pixel, Nexus, or even tablets.

3. **Select a System Image:**

   o After selecting the device, Android Studio will prompt you to choose a system image. You can choose the latest stable version of Android or any other version that suits your app's requirements. For example, you might select **Pie (API 28).**

4. **Configure Emulator Settings:**

- Customize your emulator's configuration (e.g., RAM, CPU architecture, etc.). You can also enable hardware acceleration for better performance.

5. **Finish Setup and Launch the Emulator:**

    - Once you finish configuring the virtual device, click **Finish**. You'll now see your emulator listed in the AVD Manager. Select it and click the green play button to start the emulator.

Running Your App on the Emulator

1. **Build and Run Your App:**

    - With the emulator running, click on the **Run** button (green arrow) in Android Studio. Select the emulator as the deployment target, and Android Studio will build and install the app onto the emulator.

2. **Testing on the Emulator:**

    - The emulator will launch, and you'll see your app running as it would on a real device. You can interact with your app using your mouse and keyboard, and view logs and performance data in the Logcat window.

3. **Making Changes:**

    - You can make changes to your app's code or layout and re-run it on the emulator. Android Studio will automatically detect the changes and reload the app on the emulator with the updated code.

Emulator Performance Tips

While the Android Emulator is a powerful tool, it can sometimes be slow. Here are a few tips to improve performance:

- **Enable Hardware Acceleration:** Make sure your system has hardware acceleration enabled. This can be done by configuring the AVD to use **x86** system images and enabling **Intel HAXM** (on Windows) or **Android Emulator Hypervisor Driver** (on macOS).

- **Use Quick Boot:** Android Studio supports Quick Boot, which allows the emulator to start up faster by saving and restoring the emulator state.

Conclusion

By now, you should have a solid understanding of Android Studio and how to navigate its rich set of features. From setting up your environment and understanding the project structure to running your app on the emulator, this section has equipped you with the essential knowledge to start developing Android apps. In the next sections, we will dive deeper into building apps with Kotlin, writing UI components, and connecting with backend services to create fully functional applications.

CHAPTER 3: EXPLORING KOTLIN SYNTAX FOR ANDROID DEVELOPMENT

Kotlin is a modern, statically typed language that has quickly become the language of choice for Android app development. Its succinct syntax, enhanced safety features, and compatibility with Java make it an excellent choice for building robust and efficient Android applications. In this section, we'll explore the core syntax of Kotlin, including variables, data types, constants, functions, control flow, and object-oriented programming (OOP) concepts. Whether you're a novice or an experienced developer, understanding these fundamental aspects of Kotlin is essential for becoming proficient in Android development.

3.1 Variables, Data Types, and Constants: The Building Blocks of Kotlin

3.1.1 Declaring Variables in Kotlin

In Kotlin, variables are the foundation of any program. A variable stores data, and the type of data it stores is defined by the variable's type. Kotlin uses two primary ways to declare variables: **val** and **var**.

- **val (Immutable Variable):** This keyword is used for variables whose value cannot be reassigned after initialization. Once a value is assigned, it is read-only. This is similar to a final variable in Java.

- **var (Mutable Variable):** This keyword is used for variables whose value can change. Unlike val, var allows reassignment after initialization.

kotlin

```
val pi: Double = 3.14159  // Immutable variable
var age: Int = 30  // Mutable variable
age = 31  // Allowed
```

When declaring variables, Kotlin supports **type inference**, meaning the type can often be omitted if the compiler can infer it from the assigned value. Kotlin's type inference helps make the code more concise and readable.

kotlin

```
val name = "John"  // Kotlin infers that 'name' is a String
var height = 5.9  // Kotlin infers that 'height' is a Double
```

3.1.2 Primitive Data Types in Kotlin

Kotlin uses several fundamental data types that are essential for most applications. These data types are similar to Java's primitive types but are implemented as objects under the hood, which brings additional benefits like null safety.

1. **Numeric Types:**

   o **Int:** Represents a 32-bit signed integer.

   o **Long:** Represents a 64-bit signed integer.

   o **Double:** Represents a double-precision floating-point number.

   o **Float:** Represents a single-precision floating-point number.

kotlin

```kotlin
val integerNumber: Int = 100
val largeNumber: Long = 10000000000L  // Note the 'L' suffix
val price: Double = 99.99
val temperature: Float = 32.5F  // Note the 'F' suffix
```

2. **Character and String Types:**

- o **Char**: Represents a single Unicode character.

- o **String**: Represents a sequence of characters.

kotlin

```kotlin
val letter: Char = 'A'
val message: String = "Hello, Kotlin!"
```

3. **Boolean Type:**

- o **Boolean**: Represents a logical value, either true or false.

kotlin

```kotlin
val isKotlinFun: Boolean = true
val isAdult: Boolean = age >= 18
```

3.1.3 Constants in Kotlin

In addition to mutable and immutable variables, Kotlin provides a special feature for constants. Constants are values that cannot be changed throughout the lifecycle of the program. The **const** keyword is used to define compile-time constants.

kotlin

```kotlin
const val MAX_USERS: Int = 1000  // A constant that cannot be changed
```

It's important to note that **const** can only be used with primitive types or String. This makes it different from val, which can be used with any type of object and allows for runtime initialization.

3.1.4 Nullability in Kotlin

Kotlin offers robust null safety by differentiating between nullable and non-nullable types. In Kotlin, variables cannot hold null values unless explicitly declared as nullable. You declare a nullable type by adding a **?** to the type.

kotlin

```
val nonNullableName: String = "Kotlin"  // Cannot be null
val nullableName: String? = null  // Can hold null
```

Kotlin provides several ways to safely handle nullable types, such as the **safe call operator (?.)** and the **null coalescing operator (?:)**.

kotlin

```
val length: Int? = nullableName?.length  // Safe call, returns null if
nullableName is null
val defaultLength = nullableName?.length ?: 0  // If nullableName is null,
default to 0
```

3.2 Functions and Control Flow: Writing and Using Functions, Conditional Statements, and Loops

3.2.1 Functions in Kotlin

In Kotlin, functions are first-class citizens, meaning they can be defined at the top level, inside a class, or passed as parameters. Kotlin simplifies function syntax, making it more concise compared to Java.

BASIC FUNCTION SYNTAX

To define a function in Kotlin, use the fun keyword followed by the function name, parameters, and return type. If a function does not return any value, the return type is omitted, or you can specify it as Unit (equivalent to void in Java).

kotlin

```kotlin
fun greet(name: String): String {
   return "Hello, $name!"
}
```
You can also define functions with default parameter values, making your code more flexible and easier to maintain.

kotlin

```kotlin
fun greet(name: String = "Guest"): String {
   return "Hello, $name!"
}
```

FUNCTION EXPRESSIONS

Kotlin allows you to define concise function expressions, particularly for single-expression functions. This eliminates the need for curly braces and return statements.

kotlin

```kotlin
fun greet(name: String) = "Hello, $name!"
```

3.2.2 Control Flow in Kotlin

Control flow statements in Kotlin are similar to other programming languages but with some unique features and enhancements.

CONDITIONAL STATEMENTS

Kotlin provides traditional conditional statements like if, else, and when (similar to switch in Java) for making decisions in your code.

- **if and else**: These work just as you would expect, but Kotlin allows if to return a value, making it more flexible.

kotlin

```
val result = if (age >= 18) "Adult" else "Minor"
```

- **when (Switch Statement)**: Kotlin's when is more powerful than Java's switch. It can be used as a statement or an expression that returns a value, and it supports ranges, types, and complex conditions.

kotlin

```
when (age) {
    in 0..17 -> println("Minor")
    in 18..59 -> println("Adult")
    else -> println("Senior")
}
```

LOOPS IN KOTLIN

Kotlin supports several types of loops: for, while, and do..while.

- **for Loop**: Used to iterate over ranges, arrays, or collections. Kotlin makes it very easy to loop over a range of values.

kotlin

```
for (i in 1..5) {
    println(i)  // Prints numbers 1 through 5
}
```

- **while Loop**: The while loop runs as long as a condition is true.

kotlin

```
var counter = 0
while (counter < 5) {
    println(counter)
    counter++
}
```

- **do..while Loop**: Similar to while, but guarantees that the loop will run at least once.

kotlin

```
var counter = 0
do {
    println(counter)
    counter++
} while (counter < 5)
```

3.2.3 Lambdas and Higher-Order Functions

Kotlin's support for **lambdas** and **higher-order functions** is one of the key features that sets it apart from Java. A **lambda** is a function that is defined without a name and can be passed around as a parameter.

LAMBDA EXPRESSIONS

kotlin

```
val add = { x: Int, y: Int -> x + y }
println(add(5, 3))  // Outputs: 8
```
Higher-Order Functions

A **higher-order function** is a function that takes other functions as parameters or returns a function. Kotlin makes it easy to pass functions as arguments to other functions.

kotlin

```kotlin
fun performOperation(a: Int, b: Int, operation: (Int, Int) -> Int): Int {
    return operation(a, b)
}

val result = performOperation(5, 3, add)  // Using the 'add' lambda
println(result)  // Outputs: 8
```

3.3 Object-Oriented Programming with Kotlin: Understanding Classes, Objects, Inheritance, and Polymorphism

3.3.1 Classes and Objects in Kotlin

Kotlin is an object-oriented language that supports classes, objects, inheritance, and polymorphism. It also provides features like data classes, which are specifically designed to hold data and eliminate boilerplate code.

DEFINING A CLASS

Classes in Kotlin are defined using the class keyword. You can define properties (variables) and methods (functions) inside a class.

kotlin

```kotlin
class Car(val brand: String, var speed: Int) {
    fun drive() {
        println("The $brand is driving at $speed km/h")
    }
}
```

CREATING AN OBJECT

Once you define a class, you can create an object using the new keyword in Java, but in Kotlin, creating an object is much simpler.

```kotlin
val myCar = Car("Toyota", 100)
myCar.drive() // Outputs: The Toyota is driving at 100 km/h
```

PRIMARY CONSTRUCTOR AND INITIALIZATION

In Kotlin, you can declare the class's constructor directly in the class definition, which is cleaner and reduces boilerplate code.

```kotlin
class Car(val brand: String, var speed: Int) {
    init {
        println("A new $brand car has been created!")
    }
}
```

3.3.2 Inheritance in Kotlin

Kotlin supports single inheritance (like Java) through the use of the **open** keyword. By default, all classes in Kotlin are final (non-inheritable), and to allow a class to be subclassed, you must explicitly mark it as open.

```kotlin
open class Vehicle(val brand: String) {
    open fun move() {
        println("$brand is moving")
    }
}

class Car(brand: String, val speed: Int) : Vehicle(brand) {
    override fun move() {
        println("$brand is driving at $speed km/h")
    }
}
```

In this example, Vehicle is an open class, and Car inherits from it and overrides the move() method.

3.3.3 Polymorphism in Kotlin

Polymorphism allows you to call methods on an object without knowing its exact type. Kotlin supports polymorphism through method overriding, interfaces, and abstract classes.

kotlin

```
open class Animal {
    open fun makeSound() {
        println("Some generic animal sound")
    }
}

class Dog : Animal() {
    override fun makeSound() {
        println("Bark")
    }
}

fun main() {
    val animal: Animal = Dog()
    animal.makeSound()  // Outputs: Bark
}
```

In this example, the animal reference points to a Dog object, demonstrating polymorphism. The makeSound() method is overridden in the Dog class, and it is called dynamically based on the actual object type.

Conclusion

Understanding the core syntax of Kotlin is essential for any Android developer. By mastering variables, functions, control flow, and object-oriented principles like classes, inheritance, and polymorphism, you set yourself up for building scalable and maintainable applications. Kotlin's concise syntax, null safety features, and functional programming capabilities make it a powerful tool for Android development. In the next sections, we'll explore how to leverage these fundamental concepts to build robust Android applications and optimize them for production environments.

CHAPTER 4: BUILDING USER INTERFACES (UI) IN ANDROID

User interfaces (UIs) are the backbone of any Android application. They are the point of interaction between users and the app, and crafting an intuitive, responsive, and aesthetically pleasing UI is one of the key factors in creating a successful app. In Android, building UIs involves working with **views**, **layouts**, and various **UI components** that let developers build rich, interactive experiences. This section dives deep into building UIs in Android, including an introduction to views and layouts, exploring different types of layouts like LinearLayout, RelativeLayout, and ConstraintLayout, and customizing UI components.

4.1 Introduction to Android Views and Layouts

4.1.1 What Are Views in Android?

In Android, a **view** is an object that occupies a rectangular area on the screen and is responsible for handling events such as clicks, touches, and gestures. Views are the basic building blocks for user interface components like buttons, text fields, image views, and more. Every UI component in Android is a subclass of the View class, and you can create custom views by extending this class.

Some common examples of Android views are:

- **Button**: A button element that users can click.

- **TextView**: A view used to display text.

- **EditText**: A text field used to allow users to enter input.

- **ImageView**: A view used to display an image.

CREATING VIEWS IN CODE:

In Android, views can be created programmatically or through XML. When you create views programmatically, you instantiate a view class and add it to a parent layout.

Example of creating a Button programmatically:

kotlin

```
val button = Button(this)
button.text = "Click Me"
button.setOnClickListener {
    Toast.makeText(this, "Button clicked", Toast.LENGTH_SHORT).show()
}
```

However, most Android UIs are constructed using XML, which makes the layout and component structure easier to visualize and maintain. The XML code for creating a button would look like this:

xml

```
<Button
    android:id="@+id/button"
    android:layout_width="wrap_content"
    android:layout_height="wrap_content"
    android:text="Click Me"/>
```

4.1.2 What Are Layouts in Android?

Layouts in Android define the structure and arrangement of views on the screen. They determine how views are placed relative to each other, whether in a vertical, horizontal, or grid pattern, or relative to other elements. Every view in Android must be placed within a layout, and the layout itself must be specified in XML.

Layouts can be divided into two main categories:

- **ViewGroup**: A special kind of view that can contain other views (child views). All layouts in Android are subclasses of ViewGroup, which is responsible for arranging and positioning its child views.

- **Layout Types**: Common layout types include LinearLayout, RelativeLayout, ConstraintLayout, and FrameLayout.

4.1.3 Basic Views in Android

Here are some of the basic and commonly used views that are used in most Android applications:

- **Button**: A button that can trigger actions when clicked.

xml

```
<Button
    android:id="@+id/myButton"
    android:layout_width="wrap_content"
    android:layout_height="wrap_content"
    android:text="Click Me"/>
```

- **TextView**: A simple view that displays text.

xml

```
<TextView
    android:id="@+id/myTextView"
    android:layout_width="wrap_content"
    android:layout_height="wrap_content"
    android:text="Welcome to Kotlin"/>
```

- **EditText**: A view that allows the user to input text.

xml

```xml
<EditText
    android:id="@+id/myEditText"
    android:layout_width="match_parent"
    android:layout_height="wrap_content"
    android:hint="Enter your name"/>
```

- **ImageView**: Displays an image from resources or a URL.

xml

```xml
<ImageView
    android:id="@+id/myImageView"
    android:layout_width="wrap_content"
    android:layout_height="wrap_content"
    android:src="@drawable/my_image"/>
```

These are some basic views that will be used frequently in any Android app, whether for handling user input or displaying content.

4.2 Exploring Different Layouts: LinearLayout, RelativeLayout, and ConstraintLayout

4.2.1 LinearLayout

The **LinearLayout** is one of the simplest and most widely used layouts in Android. It arranges its child views in either a vertical or horizontal sequence, based on the orientation property. This layout is often used when you want views to be aligned one after another, either in rows or columns.

HORIZONTAL VS. VERTICAL LINEARLAYOUT:

- **Vertical LinearLayout**: Places views in a single column.

xml

```xml
<LinearLayout
```

```xml
    android:orientation="vertical"
    android:layout_width="match_parent"
    android:layout_height="match_parent">

    <Button
        android:id="@+id/button1"
        android:text="Button 1"
        android:layout_width="match_parent"
        android:layout_height="wrap_content"/>

    <Button
        android:id="@+id/button2"
        android:text="Button 2"
        android:layout_width="match_parent"
        android:layout_height="wrap_content"/>
</LinearLayout>
```

- **Horizontal LinearLayout**: Places views in a single row.

xml

```xml
<LinearLayout
    android:orientation="horizontal"
    android:layout_width="match_parent"
    android:layout_height="wrap_content">

    <Button
        android:id="@+id/button1"
        android:text="Button 1"
        android:layout_width="wrap_content"
        android:layout_height="wrap_content"/>

    <Button
        android:id="@+id/button2"
        android:text="Button 2"
        android:layout_width="wrap_content"
        android:layout_height="wrap_content"/>
</LinearLayout>
```

4.2.2 RelativeLayout

The **RelativeLayout** is a more flexible layout compared to LinearLayout. It allows you to position child views relative to each other or the parent container. This makes it ideal for complex UIs where you need precise control over the placement of elements.

Using RelativeLayout:

You can position views relative to one another using attributes like android:layout_alignParentTop, android:layout_below, android:layout_toEndOf, etc.

xml

```
<RelativeLayout
    android:layout_width="match_parent"
    android:layout_height="match_parent">

    <Button
      android:id="@+id/button1"
      android:text="Top Button"
      android:layout_width="wrap_content"
      android:layout_height="wrap_content"
      android:layout_alignParentTop="true"/>

    <Button
      android:id="@+id/button2"
      android:text="Below Button"
      android:layout_width="wrap_content"
      android:layout_height="wrap_content"
      android:layout_below="@id/button1"/>
</RelativeLayout>
```

4.2.3 ConstraintLayout

The **ConstraintLayout** is one of the most powerful and flexible layouts available in Android. It allows you to create complex UIs by defining relationships between views using constraints. You can position views relative to each other, to the parent layout, or both. This layout is particularly useful for responsive and adaptive designs.

CREATING A UI WITH CONSTRAINTLAYOUT:

Unlike LinearLayout or RelativeLayout, ConstraintLayout does not have fixed orientations. Instead, you set constraints between views to determine their position relative to the parent or other sibling views.

xml

```
<androidx.constraintlayout.widget.ConstraintLayout
    android:layout_width="match_parent"
    android:layout_height="match_parent">

    <Button
       android:id="@+id/button1"
       android:text="First Button"
       android:layout_width="wrap_content"
       android:layout_height="wrap_content"
       app:layout_constraintTop_toTopOf="parent"
       app:layout_constraintStart_toStartOf="parent"/>

    <Button
       android:id="@+id/button2"
       android:text="Second Button"
       android:layout_width="wrap_content"
       android:layout_height="wrap_content"
       app:layout_constraintTop_toBottomOf="@id/button1"
       app:layout_constraintStart_toStartOf="parent"/>
</androidx.constraintlayout.widget.ConstraintLayout>
```

In this example, the buttons are positioned using constraints to ensure they are placed correctly relative to each other and to the parent.

ADVANTAGES OF CONSTRAINTLAYOUT:

- **Flexibility**: You can create complex UIs with flat view hierarchies.

- **Performance**: It is optimized for performance, reducing the need for nested layouts.

- **Responsiveness**: With constraints, it's easier to create adaptive layouts that adjust to different screen sizes.

4.3 Customizing UI Components: Styling Views and Creating Custom Components

4.3.1 Styling Views

Styling your views helps improve the aesthetics and usability of your app. In Android, styling is done using **XML** in the res/values/styles.xml file. You can define style resources that can be reused across multiple views or activities.

BASIC STYLING IN ANDROID:

xml

```
<resources>
   <style name="CustomButton">
      <item name="android:background">#FF6347</item>  <!-- Tomato color --
>
      <item name="android:textColor">#FFFFFF</item>  <!-- White text -->
      <item name="android:textSize">18sp</item>
   </style>
</resources>
```

Now, you can apply this style to a button:

xml

```
<Button
   android:id="@+id/button1"
   style="@style/CustomButton"
   android:text="Styled Button"
   android:layout_width="wrap_content"
   android:layout_height="wrap_content"/>
```

You can define different styles for different UI elements, and these can be applied to multiple views to maintain consistency throughout the app.

4.3.2 Custom Components

Creating custom UI components allows you to extend the functionality of Android views and build unique user experiences. A custom component in Android is typically created by extending an existing view, like TextView, Button, or LinearLayout, and overriding its behavior.

CREATING A CUSTOM VIEW:

kotlin

```kotlin
class CustomButton(context: Context, attrs: AttributeSet) : Button(context, attrs) {
    init {
        // Custom initialization for the button
        setBackgroundColor(Color.RED)
        setTextColor(Color.WHITE)
        textSize = 18f
    }

    override fun performClick(): Boolean {
        // Custom click behavior
        Toast.makeText(context, "Custom Button Clicked", Toast.LENGTH_SHORT).show()
        return super.performClick()
    }
}
```

In this example, the CustomButton class extends Button and modifies its properties. You can use this custom button in your layout just like any standard button.

xml

```xml
<com.example.myapp.CustomButton
    android:id="@+id/customButton"
    android:layout_width="wrap_content"
    android:layout_height="wrap_content"
    android:text="Click Me"/>
```

CREATING A CUSTOM LAYOUT:

Custom layouts are often created by extending ViewGroup and overriding its layout logic to control how children are arranged.

kotlin

```kotlin
class CustomLayout(context: Context) : ViewGroup(context) {
    override fun onLayout(p0: Boolean, p1: Int, p2: Int, p3: Int) {
        // Custom layout logic
    }
}
```

Custom views allow you to encapsulate complex UI behavior into reusable components.

Conclusion

Building user interfaces in Android involves working with various views, layouts, and UI components. Understanding the different layout types, such as LinearLayout, RelativeLayout, and ConstraintLayout, helps you create responsive and flexible UIs. Customizing views and creating custom components adds another layer of power, allowing you to build unique user experiences. Mastering these UI concepts will help you create beautiful, functional, and high-performing Android apps that users love to interact with. In the following sections, we will explore more advanced topics related to UI design, such as animation, gestures, and integrating with other Android features.

CHAPTER 5: HANDLING USER INPUT

Handling user input effectively is one of the most crucial aspects of Android app development. A well-designed app should not only be intuitive and responsive but also validate and handle user input efficiently. Whether it's a button click, text entry, or complex gestures, handling these interactions properly ensures a smooth user experience. This section dives into various ways to manage user interactions in Android, covering button clicks, text input, gestures, input validation, and working with other interactive elements like spinners, checkboxes, and radio buttons.

5.1 Managing User Interactions: Handling Button Clicks, Text Input, and Gestures

5.1.1 Handling Button Clicks

Buttons are fundamental UI components in Android. They trigger actions when clicked, such as submitting a form, navigating to another screen, or changing the state of the application. In Android, handling button clicks is straightforward, and developers have several ways to achieve this.

SETTING UP BUTTON CLICKS IN XML

The most common way to define a button in Android is through XML layout files. Each button can be assigned an OnClickListener either in XML or programmatically in Kotlin.

In XML, you can specify an onClick attribute, which links the button to a method in your activity:

xml

```
<Button
    android:id="@+id/myButton"
    android:layout_width="wrap_content"
    android:layout_height="wrap_content"
    android:text="Click Me"
    android:onClick="handleButtonClick"/>
```

In the activity, define the handleButtonClick method:

kotlin

```
fun handleButtonClick(view: View) {
    Toast.makeText(this, "Button clicked!", Toast.LENGTH_SHORT).show()
}
```

When the user clicks the button, the handleButtonClick method is invoked, and a toast message is displayed.

PROGRAMMATICALLY SETTING AN ONCLICKLISTENER

Alternatively, you can set the OnClickListener programmatically in Kotlin:

kotlin

```
val button = findViewById<Button>(R.id.myButton)
button.setOnClickListener {
    Toast.makeText(this, "Button clicked!", Toast.LENGTH_SHORT).show()
}
```

This approach is useful when you need to add dynamic behavior to buttons that are created at runtime or when working with more complex views.

5.1.2 Handling Text Input

Text input fields are commonly used in apps to capture user information, such as names, email addresses, or comments. In Android, the most widely used input view is EditText, which allows users to type text into a form field.

CREATING AND HANDLING EDITTEXT

You can create an EditText widget in XML and associate it with a variable in your activity:

xml

```xml
<EditText
    android:id="@+id/myEditText"
    android:layout_width="match_parent"
    android:layout_height="wrap_content"
    android:hint="Enter text"
    android:inputType="text"/>
```

In Kotlin, you can retrieve the text entered by the user as follows:

kotlin

```kotlin
val editText = findViewById<EditText>(R.id.myEditText)
val userInput = editText.text.toString() // Get the text input as a string
```

To handle text changes in real-time (e.g., to enable a button only when the input is valid), you can use a TextWatcher:

kotlin

```kotlin
editText.addTextChangedListener(object : TextWatcher {
    override fun afterTextChanged(s: Editable?) {
        // Called after the text has been changed
    }

    override fun beforeTextChanged(s: CharSequence?, start: Int, count: Int, after: Int) {
        // Called before the text is changed
    }
```

```
override fun onTextChanged(s: CharSequence?, start: Int, before: Int, count:
Int) {
    // Called while the text is being changed
  }
})
```

This TextWatcher gives you control over the text input, allowing you to monitor changes and react to them in real-time, which is useful for validations or enabling/disabling UI elements.

5.1.3 Gesture Handling

Gestures such as taps, swipes, pinches, and long presses can add an interactive layer to an app. In Android, gesture handling can be achieved using GestureDetector, ScaleGestureDetector, or by handling touch events directly.

SIMPLE GESTURE DETECTION

For handling simple gestures like single taps or long presses, Android provides a GestureDetector. Here's an example of detecting a tap:

kotlin

```
val gestureDetector = GestureDetector(this, object :
GestureDetector.SimpleOnGestureListener() {
    override fun onSingleTapUp(e: MotionEvent?): Boolean {
        Toast.makeText(this@MainActivity, "Single tap detected",
Toast.LENGTH_SHORT).show()
        return true
    }
})

val touchListener = View.OnTouchListener { v, event ->
    gestureDetector.onTouchEvent(event)
}

val button = findViewById<Button>(R.id.myButton)
```

button.setOnTouchListener(touchListener)

This code detects a single tap on the button and shows a toast message. You can similarly detect other gestures, such as scrolling, flinging, and long presses, using the GestureDetector methods.

HANDLING MULTI-TOUCH GESTURES

For more advanced gestures like pinch-to-zoom or multi-finger swipes, Android provides the ScaleGestureDetector, which can be used to detect scaling gestures, such as pinch-to-zoom.

kotlin

```kotlin
val scaleGestureDetector = ScaleGestureDetector(this, object :
ScaleGestureDetector.SimpleOnScaleGestureListener() {
    override fun onScale(detector: ScaleGestureDetector?): Boolean {
        val scaleFactor = detector?.scaleFactor ?: 1f
        // Handle pinch zoom here
        return true
    }
})

val touchListener = View.OnTouchListener { v, event ->
    scaleGestureDetector.onTouchEvent(event)
}

val imageView = findViewById<ImageView>(R.id.myImageView)
imageView.setOnTouchListener(touchListener)
```

This approach provides a way to handle zooming or scaling gestures within your app, enhancing the user experience.

5.2 Validating User Input: Ensuring Data Integrity and Providing Feedback to Users

5.2.1 Input Validation Basics

Input validation is a crucial part of handling user input, as it ensures that the data entered is correct and consistent. This step helps prevent errors, crashes, and incorrect data from being stored or processed.

VALIDATING TEXT INPUT

A common scenario is validating user input in text fields. For example, when a user enters an email address or phone number, you might want to validate the format of the input. Here's an example of validating an email address using a regular expression (regex):

kotlin

```kotlin
fun isValidEmail(email: String): Boolean {
    val emailRegex = "^[A-Za-z0-9+_.-]+@[A-Za-z0-9.-]+$".toRegex()
    return email.matches(emailRegex)
}

val emailInput = findViewById<EditText>(R.id.emailEditText).text.toString()
if (isValidEmail(emailInput)) {
    // Proceed with the input
} else {
    // Show an error message
    Toast.makeText(this, "Invalid email address",
Toast.LENGTH_SHORT).show()
}
```

This method checks whether the input matches the regex for an email format. If it doesn't, the app can display an error message to the user.

Similarly, numeric input can be validated by checking whether the input is a valid number. For example, you can check if a user entered a valid age or a positive integer:

kotlin

```kotlin
fun isPositiveNumber(input: String): Boolean {
    return input.toIntOrNull() != null && input.toInt() > 0
}
```

Using toIntOrNull() safely attempts to parse the input into an integer, and the validation checks if it is a positive number.

5.2.2 Providing Feedback to Users

Providing feedback to users is essential in helping them understand what they are doing right or wrong. Android offers several ways to give feedback, such as **Toast messages**, **Snackbars**, **Error messages** in text fields, and **Visual indicators** like color changes or icons.

TOAST MESSAGES

Toast messages are short, non-intrusive messages that appear on the screen for a short period. These are great for giving feedback on user actions, like clicking a button.

kotlin

```kotlin
Toast.makeText(this, "Action successful", Toast.LENGTH_SHORT).show()
```

SNACKBARS

A Snackbar is a lightweight, brief message that appears at the bottom of the screen. Unlike a Toast, it can include action buttons that allow the user to take an action.

kotlin

```kotlin
val snackbar = Snackbar.make(findViewById(R.id.coordinatorLayout), "Email saved", Snackbar.LENGTH_LONG)
snackbar.setAction("Undo") {
    // Handle the undo action
}
snackbar.show()
```

ERROR MESSAGES IN EDITTEXT

To provide immediate feedback on text input fields, you can use setError() to display an error message within the EditText widget itself.

kotlin

```kotlin
val editText = findViewById<EditText>(R.id.myEditText)
if (editText.text.isEmpty()) {
    editText.error = "This field cannot be empty"
}
```

This helps users understand exactly where their input is incorrect and gives them a clear path to resolve it.

5.3 Working with Spinners, Checkboxes, and RadioButtons: More Interactive UI Elements

5.3.1 Working with Spinners

A **Spinner** is a dropdown widget that allows users to select a value from a list of options. It's ideal when you need to limit the user's choices to a predefined set of values.

CREATING A SPINNER

Here's how you can create and handle a spinner in XML and Kotlin:

xml

```
<Spinner
    android:id="@+id/mySpinner"
    android:layout_width="wrap_content"
    android:layout_height="wrap_content" />
```

In Kotlin, you can populate the spinner with data using an ArrayAdapter:

kotlin

```
val spinner: Spinner = findViewById(R.id.mySpinner)
val options = arrayOf("Option 1", "Option 2", "Option 3")
val adapter = ArrayAdapter(this, android.R.layout.simple_spinner_item,
options)
adapter.setDropDownViewResource(android.R.layout.simple_spinner_dropdow
n_item)
spinner.adapter = adapter

spinner.onItemSelectedListener = object : AdapterView.OnItemSelectedListener
{
    override fun onItemSelected(parentView: AdapterView<*>?, view: View?,
position: Int, id: Long) {
        val selectedOption = parentView?.getItemAtPosition(position) as String
```

```
Toast.makeText(this@MainActivity, "Selected: $selectedOption",
Toast.LENGTH_SHORT).show()
  }

  override fun onNothingSelected(parentView: AdapterView<*>?) {}
}
```
This sets up a basic spinner with predefined options and handles the selection event.

5.3.2 Working with Checkboxes

Checkboxes allow users to select multiple items from a set of options. They're commonly used for forms and settings screens where users can choose multiple preferences.

CREATING A CHECKBOX

Here's how you create a checkbox in XML:

xml

```
<CheckBox
    android:id="@+id/myCheckbox"
    android:layout_width="wrap_content"
    android:layout_height="wrap_content"
    android:text="Accept Terms and Conditions" />
```

HANDLING CHECKBOX STATE

In Kotlin, you can check if the checkbox is checked or unchecked using isChecked:

kotlin

```
val checkbox = findViewById<CheckBox>(R.id.myCheckbox)
checkbox.setOnCheckedChangeListener { _, isChecked ->
    if (isChecked) {
```

```
    Toast.makeText(this, "Checkbox checked",
Toast.LENGTH_SHORT).show()
   } else {
    Toast.makeText(this, "Checkbox unchecked",
Toast.LENGTH_SHORT).show()
   }
}
```

5.3.3 Working with RadioButtons

A **RadioButton** is a UI element that allows users to select a single option from a group. Radio buttons are grouped together in a **RadioGroup**, ensuring that only one option can be selected at a time.

CREATING RADIOBUTTONS AND RADIOGROUP

Here's how you create a set of radio buttons in XML:

xml

```
<RadioGroup
    android:id="@+id/myRadioGroup"
    android:layout_width="wrap_content"
    android:layout_height="wrap_content">

    <RadioButton
        android:id="@+id/radioButton1"
        android:text="Option 1"
        android:layout_width="wrap_content"
        android:layout_height="wrap_content" />

    <RadioButton
        android:id="@+id/radioButton2"
        android:text="Option 2"
        android:layout_width="wrap_content"
        android:layout_height="wrap_content" />
</RadioGroup>
```

Handling RadioButton Selection

In Kotlin, you can detect which RadioButton is selected:

kotlin

```
val radioGroup = findViewById<RadioGroup>(R.id.myRadioGroup)
radioGroup.setOnCheckedChangeListener { _, checkedId ->
    val selectedRadioButton = findViewById<RadioButton>(checkedId)
    Toast.makeText(this, "Selected: ${selectedRadioButton.text}",
Toast.LENGTH_SHORT).show()
}
```

Conclusion

Handling user input effectively is essential for creating intuitive, responsive Android apps. Whether dealing with button clicks, text input, gestures, or more complex UI elements like spinners, checkboxes, and radio buttons, Android provides a rich set of tools for managing user interactions. Validating input ensures data integrity, while providing real-time feedback improves the user experience. By mastering these techniques, developers can create apps that are not only functional but also user-friendly and reliable. In the next sections, we will explore more advanced topics like managing complex user interactions, incorporating animations, and integrating advanced gesture controls.

CHAPTER 6: ANDROID APP LIFECYCLE AND STATE MANAGEMENT

The Android app lifecycle is a crucial concept that every Android developer must master to build responsive, efficient, and stable applications. Understanding how Android manages app activities, fragments, and states enables developers to create apps that behave predictably, handle interruptions gracefully, and provide a seamless user experience. The lifecycle governs how components like **Activities** and **Fragments** transition between different states, while state management ensures that data persists even during app interruptions such as screen rotations or app backgrounding.

This section explores the Android app lifecycle in-depth, detailing the activity and fragment lifecycles, saving and restoring app state with onSaveInstanceState(), and handling background tasks with services, AsyncTask, and background threads.

6.1 Understanding the Android App Lifecycle

The **Android app lifecycle** refers to the sequence of states that an app's components (such as activities, services, and fragments) go through as the app runs. The key to mastering app lifecycle management is understanding how Android handles these states and how you can hook into specific lifecycle events to perform tasks like saving data, releasing resources, or updating the UI.

6.1.1 The Activity Lifecycle

An **Activity** represents a single screen in your app and can go through a variety of states. These states are defined by a set of lifecycle methods that are called as the activity transitions between different states. The activity lifecycle is primarily managed by the Android system, but developers can override certain methods to perform tasks at each state transition.

ACTIVITY LIFECYCLE STATES

- **Created**: When an activity is first created, the onCreate() method is called. This is where you initialize your activity, set up the UI, and restore any saved state.

- **Started**: The activity becomes visible but isn't yet in the foreground. onStart() is called during this transition.

- **Resumed**: The activity is now in the foreground and can interact with the user. The onResume() method is called.

- **Paused**: The activity is partially obscured (e.g., when a dialog appears or another activity takes focus), but it's still visible. onPause() is called.

- **Stopped**: The activity is no longer visible. onStop() is called when the activity is fully obscured by another activity or when the app moves to the background.

- **Destroyed**: When the activity is completely removed from memory, the onDestroy() method is called.

COMMON LIFECYCLE METHODS

- **onCreate():** Called when the activity is first created. You perform one-time initialization here.

kotlin

```kotlin
override fun onCreate(savedInstanceState: Bundle?) {
    super.onCreate(savedInstanceState)
    setContentView(R.layout.activity_main)
    // Initialize your UI and other resources
}
```

- **onStart():** Called when the activity becomes visible to the user.

kotlin

```kotlin
override fun onStart() {
    super.onStart()
    // Activity is now visible to the user
}
```

- **onResume():** Called when the activity comes to the foreground and becomes interactive.

kotlin

```kotlin
override fun onResume() {
    super.onResume()
    // Activity is now in the foreground and ready to interact with the user
}
```

- **onPause():** Called when the activity is about to go into the background (partially visible).

kotlin

```kotlin
override fun onPause() {
    super.onPause()
    // Pause any ongoing tasks, such as video playback
}
```

- **onStop():** Called when the activity is no longer visible to the user.

kotlin

```kotlin
override fun onStop() {
    super.onStop()
    // Clean up resources that are no longer needed
}
```

- **onDestroy()**: Called when the activity is about to be destroyed. This is the place to release resources that are not needed anymore.

kotlin

```kotlin
override fun onDestroy() {
    super.onDestroy()
    // Release any resources or perform any clean-up work
}
```

6.1.2 The Fragment Lifecycle

A **Fragment** represents a portion of the UI within an activity and follows a similar lifecycle to that of an activity. Fragments are often used to create more modular and flexible UIs, especially on larger screen devices like tablets.

The fragment lifecycle is tightly coupled with the activity lifecycle. When the activity enters a particular state, the fragment also transitions to a corresponding state.

FRAGMENT LIFECYCLE STATES

- **onAttach()**: Called when the fragment is first attached to its activity. It's a good place to initialize resources that need the activity context.

- **onCreate()**: Called when the fragment is created. Initialization of non-UI elements happens here.

- **onCreateView()**: Called when the fragment's UI is created. This is where you inflate the fragment's layout.

- **onActivityCreated()**: Called when the activity's onCreate() method has been completed and the fragment's view hierarchy has been created.

- **onStart()**: Called when the fragment becomes visible.

- **onResume()**: Called when the fragment becomes active and the user can interact with it.

- **onPause()**: Called when the fragment is no longer in the foreground.

- **onStop()**: Called when the fragment is no longer visible.

- **onDestroyView()**: Called when the fragment's UI is destroyed.

- **onDestroy()**: Called when the fragment is no longer needed and should release resources.

- **onDetach()**: Called when the fragment is detached from its activity.

HANDLING FRAGMENT LIFECYCLE IN KOTLIN

kotlin

```kotlin
class MyFragment : Fragment() {

    override fun onCreateView(
        inflater: LayoutInflater, container: ViewGroup?,
        savedInstanceState: Bundle?
    ): View? {
        // Inflate the layout for this fragment
        return inflater.inflate(R.layout.fragment_my, container, false)
    }
```

```
override fun onPause() {
  super.onPause()
  // Pause or save any ongoing tasks
}

override fun onDestroyView() {
  super.onDestroyView()
  // Clean up resources related to the fragment's UI
}
}
```

6.1.3 Managing Activity and Fragment Transitions

When an activity or fragment is paused or stopped, it might need to retain some state for later use. The Android system calls onSaveInstanceState() to save the current state of an activity or fragment before it's stopped. The saved data can later be restored using onRestoreInstanceState() or in the onCreate() method. This helps handle cases like screen rotations or configuration changes.

6.2 Managing App State: Saving and Restoring App State with onSaveInstanceState()

One of the main challenges in Android development is managing app state, especially when the app is interrupted, such as during a screen rotation or when the app is moved to the background. The onSaveInstanceState() and onRestoreInstanceState() methods provide a way to save and restore the state of an activity or fragment.

6.2.1 onSaveInstanceState() and onRestoreInstanceState()

onSaveInstanceState() is called before an activity or fragment is destroyed or when the system is about to kill it to free resources. This method provides a Bundle object that can be used to store key-value pairs representing the state of the UI or other components.

SAVING STATE WITH ONSAVEINSTANCESTATE()

You can override onSaveInstanceState() to save any relevant state:

kotlin

```kotlin
override fun onSaveInstanceState(outState: Bundle) {
    super.onSaveInstanceState(outState)
    outState.putString("username", "john_doe") // Save a string value
    outState.putInt("score", 100) // Save an integer value
}
```

RESTORING STATE WITH ONRESTOREINSTANCESTATE()

Once the activity or fragment is recreated, you can restore the saved state in the onCreate() method or onRestoreInstanceState() method:

kotlin

```kotlin
override fun onCreate(savedInstanceState: Bundle?) {
    super.onCreate(savedInstanceState)
    if (savedInstanceState != null) {
        val username = savedInstanceState.getString("username")
        val score = savedInstanceState.getInt("score")
        // Use the restored state
    }
}
```

Alternatively, you can override onRestoreInstanceState() to restore the state:

kotlin

```kotlin
override fun onRestoreInstanceState(savedInstanceState: Bundle) {
    super.onRestoreInstanceState(savedInstanceState)
    val username = savedInstanceState.getString("username")
    val score = savedInstanceState.getInt("score")
    // Restore the saved values
}
```

6.2.2 Handling Configuration Changes

Android typically destroys and recreates activities during configuration changes, such as device rotations. This means that any data that's not explicitly saved will be lost. To prevent this, developers can manage state restoration by saving data in onSaveInstanceState() and restoring it afterward.

However, if you want to avoid unnecessary activity recreation during configuration changes, you can modify your app's behavior by using the configChanges attribute in the AndroidManifest.xml file. This prevents Android from destroying and recreating your activity on specific configuration changes, allowing you to manually handle the state:

xml

```xml
<activity android:name=".MainActivity"
    android:configChanges="orientation|keyboardHidden">
</activity>
```

6.2.3 Using ViewModels for State Management

For more complex state management, especially when dealing with configuration changes, **ViewModels** provide a more robust solution. ViewModels are part of Android's **Architecture Components** and help manage UI-related data in a lifecycle-conscious way.

kotlin

```kotlin
class MyViewModel : ViewModel() {
    val userName = MutableLiveData<String>()
    val score = MutableLiveData<Int>()
}
```

In your activity or fragment, you can observe the LiveData objects in the ViewModel:

kotlin

```kotlin
val myViewModel = ViewModelProvider(this).get(MyViewModel::class.java)
myViewModel.userName.observe(this, Observer { userName ->
    // Update UI with userName
})
```

Using ViewModels and LiveData ensures that your app's state survives configuration changes, and the UI updates automatically when the data changes.

6.3 Handling Background Tasks: Using Services, AsyncTask, and Background Threads

Handling background tasks is an essential part of building efficient Android applications. Whether it's downloading data from the internet, running a long task, or performing database operations, Android offers several ways to manage tasks in the background without blocking the main UI thread.

6.3.1 Using Services

A **Service** is a component that runs in the background to perform long-running operations. Services do not have a UI, but they can communicate with activities to report progress or return results.

CREATING A SERVICE

Here's how to define and start a simple service:

kotlin

```kotlin
class MyService : Service() {

    override fun onCreate() {
        super.onCreate()
        // Initialize resources for the service
    }

    override fun onStartCommand(intent: Intent?, flags: Int, startId: Int): Int {
        // Perform the task in the background
        return START_STICKY
    }

    override fun onBind(intent: Intent?): IBinder? {
        return null  // Not used in this example
    }

    override fun onDestroy() {
        super.onDestroy()
        // Clean up resources
    }
}
```

To start the service from an activity:

kotlin

```kotlin
val intent = Intent(this, MyService::class.java)
startService(intent)
```

6.3.2 Using AsyncTask

AsyncTask allows you to perform background tasks and publish results to the UI thread. It's commonly used for tasks like downloading data, performing network operations, or processing files in the background.

Here's an example of using AsyncTask:

kotlin

```kotlin
class DownloadTask : AsyncTask<Void, Int, String>() {

    override fun doInBackground(vararg params: Void?): String {
        // Perform background work here (e.g., downloading a file)
        return "Download complete!"
    }

    override fun onPostExecute(result: String) {
        super.onPostExecute(result)
        // Update the UI with the result
        Toast.makeText(applicationContext, result,
Toast.LENGTH_SHORT).show()
    }
}
```

To execute the task:

kotlin

```kotlin
DownloadTask().execute()
```

However, note that AsyncTask has been deprecated in recent versions of Android. It's now recommended to use ExecutorService, Kotlin Coroutines, or WorkManager for background work.

6.3.3 Using Background Threads

For long-running tasks that need more control, such as downloading large files or doing database operations, background threads can be used. Android provides several classes to manage threads, including Thread, HandlerThread, and ExecutorService.

Example using ExecutorService:

kotlin

```kotlin
val executorService = Executors.newSingleThreadExecutor()
executorService.execute {
```

```
// Perform background task
val result = performLongTask()
runOnUiThread {
    // Update UI with the result
    Toast.makeText(applicationContext, result,
Toast.LENGTH_SHORT).show()
  }
}
```

For more complex background tasks, Kotlin **Coroutines** offer a
highly efficient, easy-to-use, and powerful way to manage
background operations without the complexity of managing threads
manually.

Conclusion

Understanding the Android app lifecycle, managing app state, and
handling background tasks are fundamental skills for Android
developers. Mastering lifecycle management ensures that your app
behaves predictably, handles interruptions gracefully, and provides
a seamless user experience. By using tools like
onSaveInstanceState(), ViewModels, and services, developers can
effectively manage app state, even during configuration changes or
when running background tasks. By incorporating these techniques,
you can build robust, user-friendly, and efficient Android
applications.

CHAPTER 7: DATA STORAGE IN ANDROID

Effective data storage is a cornerstone of building reliable and user-friendly Android applications. Whether you're storing user preferences, large datasets, or application state, understanding the different options available for data storage in Android can help you choose the best solution for your app's needs. In this section, we'll explore **SharedPreferences**, **SQLite Databases**, and **Room Database**, providing a detailed look into how to work with these technologies to persist data in Android applications.

7.1 SharedPreferences: Storing Small Amounts of Data (e.g., User Settings)

SharedPreferences is one of the simplest ways to store data in Android. It is typically used for storing small amounts of data, such as user settings, preferences, or flags. SharedPreferences is a key-value storage mechanism that allows data to be saved persistently in the form of a Map structure, where each entry consists of a key-value pair. This is a straightforward solution for apps that need to store simple configurations or states that need to be preserved across app launches.

7.1.1 Basics of SharedPreferences

SharedPreferences in Android is ideal for storing primitive data types such as booleans, floats, integers, and strings. It allows for easy reading and writing of simple data, making it a popular choice for things like storing user preferences, login credentials, or app settings.

CREATING AND ACCESSING SHAREDPREFERENCES

You can access SharedPreferences using the getSharedPreferences() method. SharedPreferences can be used in two different modes:

- **MODE_PRIVATE**: The default mode where the data is private to the app and cannot be accessed by other apps.

- **MODE_WORLD_READABLE** and **MODE_WORLD_WRITEABLE**: These modes are deprecated, but they allowed apps to share data with others.

Here's a simple example of creating and accessing SharedPreferences in your app:

kotlin

```
val sharedPreferences = getSharedPreferences("userPreferences",
MODE_PRIVATE)
```

SAVING DATA TO SHAREDPREFERENCES

SharedPreferences stores data in key-value pairs. To save data, you need to use an Editor object to make changes, and then commit those changes using apply() or commit().

kotlin

```
val editor = sharedPreferences.edit()
editor.putString("username", "john_doe")
editor.putBoolean("isLoggedIn", true)
editor.putInt("userAge", 28)
editor.apply()  // Apply changes asynchronously
```

- **apply()**: Saves changes asynchronously without blocking the main thread.

- **commit()**: Saves changes synchronously, blocking the main thread, but returns a boolean to indicate whether the commit was successful.

READING DATA FROM SHAREDPREFERENCES

To read data from SharedPreferences, you can use the appropriate getX() method (such as getString(), getInt(), getBoolean()) and provide default values in case the key does not exist.

kotlin

```kotlin
val username = sharedPreferences.getString("username", "default_username")
val isLoggedIn = sharedPreferences.getBoolean("isLoggedIn", false)
val userAge = sharedPreferences.getInt("userAge", 0)
```

This ensures that if the key doesn't exist in the SharedPreferences file, a default value is returned instead of causing an error.

REMOVING DATA FROM SHAREDPREFERENCES

You can also remove data from SharedPreferences if no longer needed:

kotlin

```kotlin
val editor = sharedPreferences.edit()
editor.remove("username")
editor.apply()
```

Or clear all stored data:

kotlin

```kotlin
editor.clear()
editor.apply()
```

WHEN TO USE SHAREDPREFERENCES

SharedPreferences is suitable for:

- Storing app settings (e.g., theme preferences, language settings).

- Storing simple user information (e.g., username, email).

- Managing flags and small bits of state (e.g., whether a user has seen a tutorial).

However, it should not be used for storing large or complex data structures, such as arrays, lists, or images. For more structured or relational data, other storage solutions like SQLite or Room are recommended.

7.2 Using SQLite Databases: Introduction to SQLite for Structured Data Storage

SQLite is a lightweight, relational database management system that comes pre-installed with Android. It provides a more robust solution for storing structured data than SharedPreferences and is ideal for storing large datasets, such as records of items in a shopping cart, contacts, or any kind of structured information that needs to be queried, updated, and stored persistently.

7.2.1 Basics of SQLite

SQLite databases are file-based, meaning the data is stored in a single file, and the database engine runs directly within the Android application. The **SQLiteOpenHelper** class is typically used in Android to manage database creation, version management, and upgrading.

CREATING AN SQLITE DATABASE

To create an SQLite database in Android, you need to subclass the SQLiteOpenHelper class and override its onCreate() and onUpgrade() methods.

kotlin

```kotlin
class MyDatabaseHelper(context: Context) : SQLiteOpenHelper(context,
DATABASE_NAME, null, DATABASE_VERSION) {

    override fun onCreate(db: SQLiteDatabase?) {
        val createTableQuery = """
            CREATE TABLE userData (
                id INTEGER PRIMARY KEY AUTOINCREMENT,
                username TEXT,
                age INTEGER
            );
        """
        db?.execSQL(createTableQuery)
    }

    override fun onUpgrade(db: SQLiteDatabase?, oldVersion: Int, newVersion:
Int) {
        db?.execSQL("DROP TABLE IF EXISTS userData")
        onCreate(db)
    }

    companion object {
        private const val DATABASE_NAME = "app_database"
        private const val DATABASE_VERSION = 1
    }
}
```

- **onCreate()**: This method is used to create the database schema (tables, columns, etc.). Here, we create a userData table with columns for id, username, and age.

- **onUpgrade()**: This method is called when the database version is incremented. It is used to handle migrations, such as deleting and recreating tables when the schema changes.

INSERTING DATA INTO SQLITE DATABASE

To insert data into the database, you can use the insert() method, which inserts a new row into the specified table.

kotlin

```kotlin
val db = writableDatabase
val values = ContentValues().apply {
    put("username", "john_doe")
    put("age", 28)
}
db.insert("userData", null, values)
```

Here, ContentValues is used to hold the values to be inserted into the database. The insert() method takes the table name and the values to insert.

QUERYING DATA FROM SQLITE DATABASE

To query data from the database, use the query() method or rawQuery() for more complex queries.

kotlin

```kotlin
val db = readableDatabase
val cursor = db.query("userData", arrayOf("id", "username", "age"), null, null, null, null, null)

while (cursor.moveToNext()) {
    val id = cursor.getInt(cursor.getColumnIndex("id"))
    val username = cursor.getString(cursor.getColumnIndex("username"))
    val age = cursor.getInt(cursor.getColumnIndex("age"))
    // Use the retrieved data
}
cursor.close()
```

- **Cursor**: A Cursor is used to iterate over the result set of a query. It provides methods for getting the data from the columns of the query result.

UPDATING DATA IN SQLITE DATABASE

To update data in the database, use the update() method:

kotlin

```kotlin
val db = writableDatabase
val values = ContentValues().apply {
    put("username", "new_username")
}
db.update("userData", values, "id = ?", arrayOf("1"))
```
This updates the username of the user with id = 1.

DELETING DATA FROM SQLITE DATABASE

To delete data, use the delete() method:

kotlin

```kotlin
val db = writableDatabase
db.delete("userData", "id = ?", arrayOf("1"))
```
This deletes the row where the id is 1.

7.2.2 When to Use SQLite

SQLite is suitable for:

- Storing large amounts of structured data that needs to be queried or updated.

- Storing relational data, such as user information, orders, or inventory.

- Data that needs to be indexed or queried efficiently using SQL syntax.

- Apps that need offline data storage, as SQLite works seamlessly without a network connection.

While SQLite is powerful, it requires more effort in terms of schema management, query optimization, and migrations. For more modern solutions, **Room Database** is an abstraction layer over SQLite that simplifies data access.

7.3 Room Database: Using Room for a Modern and Efficient Approach to SQLite Databases

Room is part of Android's Architecture Components and provides an abstraction layer over SQLite. Room simplifies database interactions, reduces boilerplate code, and introduces a more structured and efficient way to access data in Android apps. It is designed to integrate seamlessly with other architecture components, such as ViewModel and LiveData, for a more modern, clean architecture.

7.3.1 Basics of Room

Room provides an easier way to work with SQLite by using **annotations** to define entities, databases, and DAO (Data Access Object) interfaces. It eliminates much of the manual SQL code, handling complex database operations for you.

DEFINING ENTITIES

An **Entity** in Room represents a table in the database. Each class annotated with @Entity corresponds to a table.

kotlin

```
@Entity(tableName = "userData")
```

```kotlin
data class User(
    @PrimaryKey(autoGenerate = true) val id: Int,
    @ColumnInfo(name = "username") val username: String,
    @ColumnInfo(name = "age") val age: Int
)
```

- **@Entity**: Marks a class as an entity (table).

- **@PrimaryKey**: Defines the primary key for the table.

- **@ColumnInfo**: Specifies column names (optional if the field name matches the column name).

DEFINING DAO (DATA ACCESS OBJECT)

A **DAO** defines methods for accessing the database. Room generates the necessary implementation based on the DAO interface.

kotlin

```kotlin
@Dao
interface UserDao {
    @Insert
    fun insert(user: User)

    @Update
    fun update(user: User)

    @Delete
    fun delete(user: User)

    @Query("SELECT * FROM userData WHERE id = :userId")
    fun getUserById(userId: Int): User
}
```

- **@Dao**: Marks the interface as a DAO.

- **@Insert, @Update, @Delete**: These annotations allow you to define simple CRUD operations without writing SQL.

- **@Query**: Allows you to define custom SQL queries.

CREATING THE ROOM DATABASE

To create the Room database, you define an abstract class that extends RoomDatabase. This class will be used to access the DAO.

kotlin

```kotlin
@Database(entities = [User::class], version = 1)
abstract class AppDatabase : RoomDatabase() {
    abstract fun userDao(): UserDao
}
```

- **@Database**: Specifies the entities and version of the database.

- **Room.databaseBuilder()**: Used to create or access the database.

kotlin

```kotlin
val db = Room.databaseBuilder(applicationContext, AppDatabase::class.java,
"app_database").build()
```

USING ROOM IN YOUR APP

Room provides a simple and efficient way to store, query, and update data in the database. You can easily interact with Room using DAO methods.

kotlin

```kotlin
val userDao = db.userDao()
val user = User(0, "john_doe", 28)
userDao.insert(user)
val retrievedUser = userDao.getUserById(1)
```

ROOM WITH LIVEDATA AND VIEWMODEL

Room integrates seamlessly with LiveData and ViewModel to provide an observable, lifecycle-aware data stream that automatically updates the UI.

kotlin

```kotlin
class UserRepository(private val userDao: UserDao) {
    val allUsers: LiveData<List<User>> = userDao.getAllUsers()
}

class UserViewModel(application: Application) :
AndroidViewModel(application) {
    private val repository: UserRepository
    val allUsers: LiveData<List<User>>

    init {
        val userDao = AppDatabase.getDatabase(application).userDao()
        repository = UserRepository(userDao)
        allUsers = repository.allUsers
    }
}
```

- **LiveData**: A lifecycle-aware data holder that automatically updates the UI when data changes.

- **ViewModel**: Stores and manages UI-related data in a lifecycle-conscious way.

7.3.2 When to Use Room

Room is suitable for:

- Apps that require a more structured and type-safe approach to database management.

- Apps that need to manage complex data, such as user profiles, products, or tasks, in a persistent and scalable manner.

- Apps that need to take advantage of SQLite's powerful querying capabilities while minimizing boilerplate code.

- Projects that use modern Android architecture components like LiveData and ViewModel for clean separation of concerns and lifecycle management.

Room is the recommended solution for most Android apps that need local data storage, as it simplifies the process of managing a SQLite database and offers a more modern approach to database interaction.

Conclusion

Choosing the right data storage solution in Android depends on your app's requirements. **SharedPreferences** is great for storing simple, lightweight data such as user preferences or flags. **SQLite** provides a robust relational database solution for apps that need to store and query structured data. **Room** is a modern abstraction layer over SQLite that simplifies database interactions, integrates seamlessly with other Android architecture components, and reduces boilerplate code.

Mastering these data storage solutions ensures that your Android apps can efficiently manage data, whether it's small settings or large datasets, and remain performant, reliable, and user-friendly.

CHAPTER 8: INTEGRATING APIS AND WEB SERVICES

In modern Android development, integrating external data and services is essential for creating dynamic, feature-rich applications. Whether it's fetching data from a server, interacting with third-party services, or updating content in real time, making API calls is a core aspect of building any robust Android app. This section delves deep into working with **RESTful APIs**, parsing **JSON data**, and simplifying network requests using the **Retrofit library**.

We'll start with the basics of making network requests, cover the nuances of JSON parsing to convert raw data into Kotlin objects, and explore how Retrofit can significantly streamline the process of interacting with APIs in Android applications.

8.1 Making Network Requests: Introduction to Working with RESTful APIs

8.1.1 What is a RESTful API?

A **RESTful API** (Representational State Transfer) is an architectural style for designing networked applications. It uses standard HTTP methods (GET, POST, PUT, DELETE) to perform operations on resources, which are identified using URLs. RESTful APIs are stateless, meaning each request from the client to the server must contain all the necessary information to understand and process the request.

When working with Android, interacting with a RESTful API typically involves sending HTTP requests to retrieve or manipulate data on a server, which is then parsed and displayed in your app. These requests often return data in **JSON** or **XML** format, with JSON being the most common for RESTful APIs.

8.1.2 Understanding HTTP Methods

The four main HTTP methods used in a RESTful API are:

- **GET**: Retrieves data from the server. This is the most common HTTP method used in API interactions.

- **POST**: Sends data to the server to create a new resource.

- **PUT**: Sends data to the server to update an existing resource.

- **DELETE**: Deletes a resource on the server.

Each of these methods is used in different scenarios. For example, fetching user data from a remote server would typically use a GET request, while submitting a new form might involve a POST request.

8.1.3 Making Network Requests in Android

Android provides several ways to make HTTP requests, including using libraries like HttpURLConnection, OkHttp, and Retrofit. Here, we'll focus on the process of making basic network requests and parsing the response.

Using HttpURLConnection

HttpURLConnection is Android's built-in HTTP client for making network requests. Below is an example of using HttpURLConnection to make a simple GET request to a RESTful API.

kotlin

```kotlin
val url = URL("https://api.example.com/data")
val urlConnection = url.openConnection() as HttpURLConnection
try {
    val inputStream =
BufferedReader(InputStreamReader(urlConnection.inputStream))
    val response = StringBuilder()
    var inputLine: String?
    while (inputStream.readLine().also { inputLine = it } != null) {
        response.append(inputLine)
    }
    // Handle the response here
    val responseData = response.toString()
} finally {
    urlConnection.disconnect()
}
```

This is a basic implementation using HttpURLConnection, but it requires boilerplate code for error handling, network threading, and data parsing, which is why libraries like **Retrofit** and **OkHttp** are preferred in modern Android apps.

8.2 JSON Parsing: Converting JSON Data to Kotlin Objects

8.2.1 What is JSON?

JSON (JavaScript Object Notation) is a lightweight data interchange format that is easy for humans to read and write and easy for machines to parse and generate. JSON is the most common format for responses from RESTful APIs, and it's structured as key-value pairs.

A typical JSON response might look like this:

json

```
{
  "id": 1,
  "name": "John Doe",
  "email": "john.doe@example.com"
}
```

In order to work with this data in an Android app, you need to parse the JSON and map it to Kotlin objects.

8.2.2 Parsing JSON in Kotlin

Android provides several ways to parse JSON data, but the most popular approaches are using **JSONObject** or a third-party library like **Gson** or **Moshi**. These libraries allow you to convert raw JSON into Kotlin data classes in an efficient, type-safe manner.

USING JSONOBJECT TO PARSE JSON

The Android SDK includes a JSONObject class, which can be used to manually parse JSON data. However, this approach requires you to manually extract each value from the JSON response.

kotlin

```
val jsonResponse = "{ \"id\": 1, \"name\": \"John Doe\", \"email\":
\"john.doe@example.com\" }"
val jsonObject = JSONObject(jsonResponse)
val id = jsonObject.getInt("id")
val name = jsonObject.getString("name")
val email = jsonObject.getString("email")

val user = User(id, name, email)
```

While this works, manually parsing JSON is error-prone, especially when dealing with more complex objects. Therefore, we turn to libraries like **Gson** for automatic mapping between JSON and Kotlin objects.

USING GSON FOR AUTOMATIC JSON PARSING

Gson is a popular library for converting Java/Kotlin objects to JSON and vice versa. It simplifies the parsing process and reduces boilerplate code.

First, add the Gson dependency in your build.gradle file:

gradle

```
implementation 'com.google.code.gson:gson:2.8.8'
```
Then, define a Kotlin data class to represent the JSON structure:

kotlin

```kotlin
data class User(
    val id: Int,
    val name: String,
    val email: String
)
```
You can then use Gson to automatically parse the JSON into a Kotlin object:

kotlin

```kotlin
val gson = Gson()
val user = gson.fromJson(jsonResponse, User::class.java)
```
This approach eliminates the need for manual parsing and makes the code more maintainable.

8.3 Retrofit Library

8.3.1 What is Retrofit?

Retrofit is a type-safe HTTP client for Android and Java, developed by Square. It simplifies the process of interacting with RESTful APIs by automating the task of making network requests, converting JSON into Kotlin objects, and handling responses. Retrofit integrates seamlessly with **Gson** (or **Moshi**) for parsing JSON, making it a highly popular choice for modern Android apps.

8.3.2 Setting Up Retrofit in Your Android Project

To use Retrofit in your project, you need to add the Retrofit dependency in your build.gradle file:

gradle

```
implementation 'com.squareup.retrofit2:retrofit:2.9.0'
implementation 'com.squareup.retrofit2:converter-gson:2.9.0'
```

Retrofit uses **Converters** to handle the serialization and deserialization of data. By default, Retrofit can work with Gson, but you can configure it to use other converters like Moshi, Jackson, or ProtoBuf.

8.3.3 Defining a Retrofit Interface

Retrofit simplifies the process of making API calls by allowing you to define a **Java interface** (or Kotlin interface) to represent the API endpoints. Each method in the interface corresponds to an HTTP request, and you use annotations to specify the type of request (GET, POST, PUT, DELETE) and parameters.

DEFINING THE API INTERFACE

Here's how you define a Retrofit interface for a RESTful API:

kotlin

```
interface ApiService {
    @GET("users/{id}")
    suspend fun getUser(@Path("id") userId: Int): Response<User>
```

```kotlin
@POST("users")
suspend fun createUser(@Body user: User): Response<User>
}
```

- **@GET**, **@POST**, **@PUT**, **@DELETE**: These annotations define the HTTP methods for the API endpoints.

- **@Path**: This annotation is used to pass dynamic data to the endpoint, like the userId.

- **@Body**: This annotation is used to pass an object as the body of the request (used for POST, PUT requests).

- **suspend**: The suspend keyword indicates that this function is a coroutine, making it compatible with Kotlin coroutines for asynchronous network calls.

CREATING THE RETROFIT INSTANCE

To make network requests, you need to create an instance of the Retrofit object, configure it with the base URL, and specify the converter (Gson in this case) to parse JSON data.

```kotlin
val retrofit = Retrofit.Builder()
    .baseUrl("https://api.example.com/")
    .addConverterFactory(GsonConverterFactory.create())
    .build()

val apiService = retrofit.create(ApiService::class.java)
```

8.3.4 Making API Calls with Retrofit

Retrofit provides a simple way to make API calls. You can make synchronous or asynchronous calls, but with Kotlin, we typically use coroutines for asynchronous tasks to avoid blocking the main thread.

Here's an example of using Retrofit to make an asynchronous API call:

kotlin

```kotlin
// Inside a CoroutineScope (e.g., ViewModel or Activity)
val response = apiService.getUser(userId)

if (response.isSuccessful) {
    val user = response.body()
    // Use the user object
} else {
    // Handle error response
}
```
In the code above:

- **getUser(userId)**: Makes the API call to retrieve user data.

- **response.isSuccessful**: Checks if the request was successful.

- **response.body()**: Gets the response body, which is automatically converted to the User data class.

8.3.5 Handling API Errors

One of the key advantages of Retrofit is its ability to handle API errors gracefully. By checking the response.isSuccessful flag, you can determine if the request was successful or if an error occurred. Retrofit also provides error handling using the Throwable object.

Example:

kotlin

```kotlin
try {
```

```kotlin
    val response = apiService.getUser(userId)
    if (response.isSuccessful) {
        val user = response.body()
        // Handle success
    } else {
        // Handle API error
        Log.e("API", "Error: ${response.errorBody()?.string()}")
    }
} catch (e: Exception) {
    // Handle network or other errors
    Log.e("API", "Exception: ${e.message}")
}
```

This ensures that your app can handle scenarios like network issues, timeouts, or invalid responses without crashing.

8.3.6 Handling Multipart Requests with Retrofit

Sometimes you need to send files, such as images or documents, to a server. Retrofit makes this process easy using **multipart** requests. For example, uploading an image file might require a POST request with Multipart data.

Example of sending an image:

kotlin

```kotlin
interface ApiService {
    @Multipart
    @POST("upload")
    suspend fun uploadImage(
        @Part file: MultipartBody.Part,
        @Part("description") description: RequestBody
    ): Response<UploadResponse>
}
```
You can create the MultipartBody.Part and RequestBody from files or strings like this:

kotlin

```kotlin
val file = File(filePath)
```

```
val requestBody = RequestBody.create(MediaType.parse("image/jpeg"), file)
val part = MultipartBody.Part.createFormData("file", file.name, requestBody)
val description = RequestBody.create(MediaType.parse("text/plain"), "image
description")

val response = apiService.uploadImage(part, description)
```

Conclusion

Integrating APIs and web services is a fundamental skill for Android developers, as it enables apps to interact with external data and services. By understanding the principles of RESTful APIs, parsing JSON data, and leveraging powerful libraries like Retrofit, developers can simplify the process of making network requests and handling responses. Retrofit, in particular, is a game-changer for Android developers, offering a clean, efficient, and type-safe way to manage API calls, parse JSON, and handle errors. Whether you're fetching user data, uploading files, or performing other network tasks, mastering these techniques will significantly enhance the capabilities of your Android applications.

CHAPTER 9: WORKING WITH FIREBASE

Firebase, Google's mobile platform, provides a suite of tools and services to help developers build high-quality applications. Whether you're looking to authenticate users, store and sync data in real time, or send push notifications, Firebase has you covered. Its wide range of products allows for seamless integration into your Android app, helping you to focus on building great features without worrying about server-side infrastructure.

In this section, we'll dive deep into **Firebase Authentication**, **Firebase Realtime Database**, and **Firebase Cloud Messaging**, providing you with a comprehensive understanding of how to use these tools effectively. We'll cover everything from setup to advanced usage scenarios to help you create robust, responsive apps.

9.1 Firebase Authentication: Setting Up User Authentication with Firebase

9.1.1 Introduction to Firebase Authentication

Firebase Authentication is a powerful service that provides backend services to help authenticate users, including simple pass-through authentication, third-party providers like Google and Facebook, and even anonymous logins. With Firebase Authentication, you can easily set up secure, scalable user authentication for your Android apps without needing to manage complex authentication systems yourself.

Firebase Authentication supports multiple sign-in methods, including:

- **Email/Password Authentication**: Basic email and password-based login.

- **Social Login**: Integrations with social providers like Google, Facebook, Twitter, etc.

- **Phone Authentication**: Using SMS to authenticate users.

- **Anonymous Authentication**: Allowing users to interact with the app without creating an account, with an option to upgrade to a full account later.

9.1.2 Setting Up Firebase Authentication in Your Project

To get started with Firebase Authentication in Android, follow these steps:

1. **Add Firebase to Your Android Project**:

   - Go to the Firebase Console (https://console.firebase.google.com/), create a new project, and add your Android app to the Firebase project by following the setup steps in the Firebase Console.

   - Download the google-services.json file from Firebase and add it to the app directory of your Android project.

2. **Add Dependencies**: In your app's build.gradle file, add the necessary Firebase dependencies:

gradle

```
dependencies {
    implementation 'com.google.firebase:firebase-auth:21.0.1'
    implementation 'com.google.firebase:firebase-core:19.0.1'
}
```

Then sync your project.

3. **Enable Authentication Methods**: In the Firebase Console, navigate to the **Authentication** section and enable the sign-in methods you wish to support (email/password, Google, Facebook, etc.).

9.1.3 Email and Password Authentication

The simplest form of authentication is using a user's email and password. Firebase Authentication handles storing and securing passwords, ensuring that they are encrypted and safe.

CREATING A NEW USER

Here's how you can create a new user with email and password:

kotlin

```
val auth = FirebaseAuth.getInstance()
auth.createUserWithEmailAndPassword("user@example.com", "password123")
    .addOnCompleteListener { task ->
        if (task.isSuccessful) {
            // User created successfully
            val user = auth.currentUser
            Toast.makeText(this, "User created: ${user?.email}",
Toast.LENGTH_SHORT).show()
        } else {
            // Handle error
```

```kotlin
        Toast.makeText(this, "Error: ${task.exception?.message}",
Toast.LENGTH_SHORT).show()
    }
  }
```

SIGNING IN WITH EMAIL AND PASSWORD

For users who already have an account, you can sign them in with their credentials:

kotlin

```kotlin
auth.signInWithEmailAndPassword("user@example.com", "password123")
    .addOnCompleteListener { task ->
      if (task.isSuccessful) {
        val user = auth.currentUser
        // User signed in successfully
        Toast.makeText(this, "Signed in as: ${user?.email}",
Toast.LENGTH_SHORT).show()
      } else {
        // Handle error
        Toast.makeText(this, "Error: ${task.exception?.message}",
Toast.LENGTH_SHORT).show()
      }
    }
```

SIGNING OUT

To sign out a user:

kotlin

```kotlin
auth.signOut()
```

9.1.4 Social Logins: Google Sign-In Example

Firebase makes integrating with third-party authentication providers like Google quick and easy.

1. **Set up Google Sign-In in the Firebase Console** and enable it under **Authentication > Sign-In method**.

2. **Integrate Google Sign-In SDK**: Add the dependencies for Google Sign-In:

gradle

```
implementation 'com.google.android.gms:play-services-auth:20.1.0'
```

3. **Authenticate Using Google Sign-In**:

kotlin

```
// Configure Google Sign-In
val gso =
GoogleSignInOptions.Builder(GoogleSignInOptions.DEFAULT_SIGN_IN)
    .requestIdToken(getString(R.string.default_web_client_id)) // Your web client ID
    .requestEmail()
    .build()

val googleSignInClient = GoogleSignIn.getClient(this, gso)

// Start the Google Sign-In Intent
val signInIntent = googleSignInClient.signInIntent
startActivityForResult(signInIntent, RC_SIGN_IN)
```

4. **Handle the Result:**

In onActivityResult, authenticate with Firebase:

kotlin

```
override fun onActivityResult(requestCode: Int, resultCode: Int, data: Intent?) {
    super.onActivityResult(requestCode, resultCode, data)

    if (requestCode == RC_SIGN_IN) {
        val task = GoogleSignIn.getSignedInAccountFromIntent(data)
        try {
            val account = task.getResult(ApiException::class.java)
            val credential = GoogleAuthProvider.getCredential(account.idToken, null)
            FirebaseAuth.getInstance().signInWithCredential(credential)
```

```kotlin
        .addOnCompleteListener { task ->
          if (task.isSuccessful) {
            val user = FirebaseAuth.getInstance().currentUser
            // Handle signed-in user
          } else {
            // Handle error
          }
        }
    } catch (e: ApiException) {
      // Handle sign-in error
    }
  }
}
```

9.1.5 Firebase Authentication with Phone Numbers

Phone number authentication is another popular method in Firebase Authentication. Firebase uses SMS to authenticate users.

To enable phone number authentication, go to the **Authentication** section of the Firebase console and enable **Phone Authentication**.

Here's how to implement it:

1. **Send Verification Code**:

kotlin

```kotlin
val phoneNumber = "+1234567890"
val options = PhoneAuthOptions.newBuilder(firebaseAuth)
    .setPhoneNumber(phoneNumber)      // Phone number to verify
    .setTimeout(60L, TimeUnit.SECONDS) // Timeout duration
    .setActivity(this)                // Current activity
    .setCallbacks(object :
PhoneAuthProvider.OnVerificationStateChangedCallbacks() {
        override fun onVerificationCompleted(credential: PhoneAuthCredential) {
          // Handle verification completed
        }

        override fun onVerificationFailed(e: FirebaseException) {
          // Handle failure
```

```
    }
})
 .build()
PhoneAuthProvider.verifyPhoneNumber(options)
```

2. **Verify the Code:**

kotlin

```kotlin
val credential = PhoneAuthProvider.getCredential(verificationId, code)
firebaseAuth.signInWithCredential(credential)
   .addOnCompleteListener { task ->
     if (task.isSuccessful) {
        val user = firebaseAuth.currentUser
        // Handle user login
     } else {
        // Handle error
     }
   }
}
```

9.2 Firebase Realtime Database: Storing and Syncing Data in Real-Time

9.2.1 Introduction to Firebase Realtime Database

Firebase Realtime Database is a cloud-hosted NoSQL database that allows data to be stored as JSON and synced in real-time across all clients. This means that any changes made to the data on one client are instantly reflected on all other connected clients. It is especially useful for building apps that need to reflect live changes, like chat apps, collaborative apps, or social apps.

The Firebase Realtime Database automatically handles syncing data across devices, ensuring that all clients stay up to date.

9.2.2 Setting Up Firebase Realtime Database

1. **Enable Firebase Realtime Database**:

   o   In the Firebase Console, navigate to **Realtime Database** and create a new database.

2. **Add Firebase Dependencies**:

gradle

implementation 'com.google.firebase:firebase-database:20.0.3'

3. **Get a Database Reference**:

To read and write data, you need to get a reference to the database:

kotlin

```kotlin
val database = FirebaseDatabase.getInstance()
val myRef = database.getReference("message")
```

4. **Writing Data to the Database**:

kotlin

```kotlin
val message = "Hello, Firebase!"
myRef.setValue(message)
```

This writes the value of message to the database under the path "message."

5. **Reading Data from the Database**:

kotlin

```kotlin
myRef.addValueEventListener(object : ValueEventListener {
    override fun onDataChange(snapshot: DataSnapshot) {
        val message = snapshot.getValue(String::class.java)
        println(message) // Outputs the data from the database
    }

    override fun onCancelled(error: DatabaseError) {
        // Handle possible errors
```

```
    }
})
```

9.2.3 Real-Time Syncing with Firebase Realtime Database

One of the key features of Firebase Realtime Database is its ability to sync data across all connected clients in real time. When you update data on one device, the changes are automatically pushed to all other connected devices.

Here's an example of how you can listen for real-time changes:

kotlin

```kotlin
val messagesRef = database.getReference("messages")

messagesRef.addChildEventListener(object : ChildEventListener {
    override fun onChildAdded(snapshot: DataSnapshot, previousChildName: String?) {
        val message = snapshot.getValue(String::class.java)
        // Display new message
    }

    override fun onChildChanged(snapshot: DataSnapshot, previousChildName: String?) {
        // Handle changes
    }

    override fun onChildRemoved(snapshot: DataSnapshot) {
        // Handle removed messages
    }

    override fun onChildMoved(snapshot: DataSnapshot, previousChildName: String?) {
        // Handle moved messages
    }

    override fun onCancelled(error: DatabaseError) {
        // Handle errors
    }
})
```

This listener will be triggered whenever data in the messages node changes, making it perfect for applications that need to display live updates.

9.3 Firebase Cloud Messaging: Sending Push Notifications to Users

9.3.1 Introduction to Firebase Cloud Messaging

Firebase Cloud Messaging (FCM) allows you to send notifications and data messages to users' devices. It supports both **foreground** and **background** notifications, enabling you to engage users with timely information, reminders, or updates.

With FCM, you can target users based on their behavior, segment them based on specific events, or even send notifications to a single device or a group of devices.

9.3.2 Setting Up Firebase Cloud Messaging

1. **Enable FCM in Firebase Console**:

   o   Go to the Firebase Console, select **Cloud Messaging**, and enable FCM for your project.

2. **Add FCM Dependencies**:

gradle

implementation 'com.google.firebase:firebase-messaging:23.0.0'
3. **Get the FCM Token**:

To send a notification to a specific device, you need the **device token**, which can be obtained like this:

kotlin

```
FirebaseMessaging.getInstance().token.addOnCompleteListener { task ->
    if (!task.isSuccessful) {
        Log.w("FCM", "Fetching FCM registration token failed", task.exception)
        return@addOnCompleteListener
    }

    val token = task.result
    Log.d("FCM", "FCM Token: $token")
}
```

9.3.3 Sending Push Notifications

FCM provides a simple way to send notifications using the Firebase Console or programmatically via the Firebase Admin SDK. Here's an example of how to send a notification programmatically:

kotlin

```
val message =
RemoteMessage.Builder("your_sender_id@gcm.googleapis.com")
    .setMessageId("1")
    .addData("title", "Hello!")
    .addData("message", "You have a new notification.")
    .build()

FirebaseMessaging.getInstance().send(message)
```

This sends a data-only message (without a notification) to the target device.

9.3.4 Handling Notifications in the App

To handle notifications in the app, you can implement a service that listens for incoming messages:

kotlin

```kotlin
class MyFirebaseMessagingService : FirebaseMessagingService() {

    override fun onMessageReceived(remoteMessage: RemoteMessage) {
        if (remoteMessage.data.isNotEmpty()) {
            val title = remoteMessage.data["title"]
            val message = remoteMessage.data["message"]
            // Handle the data message here
        }

        if (remoteMessage.notification != null) {
            val notificationTitle = remoteMessage.notification?.title
            val notificationBody = remoteMessage.notification?.body
            // Show a notification to the user
        }
    }
}
```

9.3.5 Background Handling and Notification Channels

FCM also allows you to handle notifications in the background, especially on Android devices running Android 8.0 (Oreo) and above. This requires setting up **notification channels** to ensure notifications are categorized properly.

kotlin

```kotlin
if (Build.VERSION.SDK_INT >= Build.VERSION_CODES.O) {
    val channel = NotificationChannel(
        "my_channel_id",
        "My Channel",
        NotificationManager.IMPORTANCE_DEFAULT
    )
    val notificationManager =
getSystemService(Context.NOTIFICATION_SERVICE) as
NotificationManager
    notificationManager.createNotificationChannel(channel)
}
```

Conclusion

Firebase offers a powerful set of tools that help developers add sophisticated features like user authentication, real-time data synchronization, and push notifications to their Android apps. By integrating **Firebase Authentication**, **Firebase Realtime Database**, and **Firebase Cloud Messaging**, developers can build apps that are not only feature-rich but also scalable and responsive. Whether you're building a social media app, an e-commerce app, or a gaming app, Firebase's seamless integration with Android ensures that you can focus more on building great features and less on the infrastructure that supports them.

CHAPTER 10: ADVANCED UI DESIGN AND ANIMATIONS

Creating stunning and engaging user interfaces (UIs) is a key aspect of mobile app development. On Android, UI design and animations go beyond just the look and feel of the app — they directly impact user experience (UX), helping apps stand out in a competitive market. As developers, we are tasked with crafting responsive, visually appealing UIs that respond intuitively to user input, and smooth animations that keep users engaged.

This section explores **Advanced UI Design and Animations** in Android, diving deep into three critical areas:

1. **Custom Views and Widgets**: How to create reusable and customizable UI components for your app.

2. **Material Design Components**: Integrating Google's Material Design principles to enhance app aesthetics and usability.

3. **Animations in Android**: How to add interactivity, smooth transitions, and engaging animations to your app.

We'll begin with custom views and widgets, proceed to the use of Material Design components, and finish with advanced animation techniques to make your app come to life.

10.1 Custom Views and Widgets: Creating Reusable and Customizable UI Components

10.1.1 Why Custom Views and Widgets?

Custom views and widgets are integral when you need a UI component that cannot be easily achieved with Android's standard UI elements. While Android provides a rich set of built-in views (like Button, TextView, ImageView), sometimes your app might require a unique UI element that combines different behaviors, looks, or interactions.

Custom views and widgets are necessary when:

- You need to combine existing views into a single, reusable component.

- You want to implement new features or behavior that aren't available with standard Android views.

- You need to optimize performance for certain UI patterns that require specialized rendering.

10.1.2 Building Custom Views

To create a custom view in Android, you need to extend the View class or any of its subclasses (like TextView, Button, etc.). Here's a step-by-step process to create a simple custom view.

1. CREATE A NEW CLASS FOR THE CUSTOM VIEW

You start by extending View, overriding the onDraw() method, and handling user interaction (like touch events) by overriding onTouchEvent().

kotlin

```kotlin
class CustomCircleView(context: Context, attrs: AttributeSet) : View(context,
attrs) {

    private val paint = Paint()

    init {
        paint.color = Color.RED
        paint.isAntiAlias = true
    }

    override fun onDraw(canvas: Canvas) {
        super.onDraw(canvas)
        val width = width
        val height = height
        val radius = Math.min(width, height) / 2f
        canvas.drawCircle(width / 2f, height / 2f, radius, paint)
    }
}
```

This custom view draws a red circle in the middle of its parent container. The onDraw() method is where all the drawing operations are done, and you can use the Canvas and Paint objects to create the visual elements.

2. CUSTOMIZING WITH XML ATTRIBUTES

To make your custom view configurable via XML (allowing users to customize it from the layout file), you can define custom XML attributes.

kotlin

```kotlin
val a = context.theme.obtainStyledAttributes(
    attrs,
    R.styleable.CustomCircleView,
    0, 0
)

val circleColor = a.getColor(R.styleable.CustomCircleView_circleColor,
Color.RED)
```

```
paint.color = circleColor
a.recycle()
```
Then, in your res/values/attrs.xml file, you would define the attributes that can be customized:

xml

```xml
<declare-styleable name="CustomCircleView">
   <attr name="circleColor" format="color"/>
</declare-styleable>
```
And finally, you can use your custom view in XML layouts:

xml

```xml
<com.example.myapp.CustomCircleView
   android:layout_width="200dp"
   android:layout_height="200dp"
   app:circleColor="#00FF00"/>
```

3. HANDLING TOUCH EVENTS

To make your custom view interactive, you can handle touch events such as clicks, drags, or gestures. Overriding the onTouchEvent() method lets you define custom behavior when the user interacts with the view.

kotlin

```kotlin
override fun onTouchEvent(event: MotionEvent): Boolean {
   when (event.action) {
     MotionEvent.ACTION_DOWN -> {
        paint.color = Color.BLUE  // Change color on touch
        invalidate()  // Redraw the view
     }
   }
   return true
}
```

10.1.3 Creating Custom Widgets

Widgets in Android are often used for creating UI components that interact with the user, such as custom buttons, sliders, or input fields. The approach to creating widgets is similar to that of creating views, but widgets usually involve managing a combination of multiple UI elements.

For example, if you want to create a custom ToggleButton that shows different images when toggled:

kotlin

```kotlin
class ImageToggleButton(context: Context, attrs: AttributeSet) :
LinearLayout(context, attrs) {
    private val imageView: ImageView
    private val textView: TextView

    init {
        inflate(context, R.layout.view_image_toggle_button, this)
        imageView = findViewById(R.id.imageView)
        textView = findViewById(R.id.textView)
    }

    fun toggleState(isActive: Boolean) {
        if (isActive) {
            imageView.setImageResource(R.drawable.ic_active)
            textView.text = "Active"
        } else {
            imageView.setImageResource(R.drawable.ic_inactive)
            textView.text = "Inactive"
        }
    }
}
```

With this custom widget, you can easily toggle between two states and update the UI in your layout. The custom widget becomes reusable and can be used across different parts of your app.

10.2 Material Design Components: Using Material Design to Improve App Appearance and Usability

10.2.1 What is Material Design?

Material Design is a design language developed by Google that combines rich visual elements with intuitive user interactions. It's a comprehensive guide that covers layout, animation, motion, and interaction patterns. Material Design components are built to look good, feel responsive, and work well on any Android device.

Material Design encourages designers and developers to create consistent, aesthetically pleasing, and accessible UIs. By adhering to the guidelines, you ensure that your app feels modern and user-friendly while maintaining design consistency.

10.2.2 Using Material Components in Android

Material Components are pre-built UI elements that follow Material Design principles. To get started with Material Components in your Android project, ensure you have the right dependencies in your build.gradle file:

gradle

```
implementation 'com.google.android.material:material:1.4.0'
```

Some of the most commonly used Material Design components include **Buttons, Text Fields, Cards, Snackbars, Dialogs**, and **Floating Action Buttons (FAB)**.

MATERIAL BUTTONS

Material Buttons are highly customizable and can be styled to match the app's branding. Here's how to create a simple MaterialButton in XML:

xml

```xml
<com.google.android.material.button.MaterialButton
    android:id="@+id/myButton"
    android:layout_width="wrap_content"
    android:layout_height="wrap_content"
    android:text="Click Me"
    app:icon="@drawable/ic_button_icon"
    app:iconGravity="textStart"
    app:cornerRadius="16dp"/>
```

This button supports icons, rounded corners, and can be easily customized to fit your design.

TEXT FIELDS

Material Design provides the **TextInputLayout** and **TextInputEditText** components for text input. These components display floating labels and provide a clean, intuitive user experience.

xml

```xml
<com.google.android.material.textfield.TextInputLayout
    android:layout_width="match_parent"
    android:layout_height="wrap_content"
    android:hint="Email">

    <com.google.android.material.textfield.TextInputEditText
        android:layout_width="match_parent"
        android:layout_height="wrap_content"
        android:inputType="textEmailAddress"/>
</com.google.android.material.textfield.TextInputLayout>
```

This creates a text input field with a floating label and an email-specific keyboard.

FLOATING ACTION BUTTON (FAB)

The **Floating Action Button** is a circular button that floats above the UI, providing quick access to important actions. It's commonly used for actions like adding new items, composing messages, or starting a new task.

xml

```
<com.google.android.material.floatingactionbutton.FloatingActionButton
    android:id="@+id/fab"
    android:layout_width="wrap_content"
    android:layout_height="wrap_content"
    android:src="@drawable/ic_add"
    app:layout_anchor="@id/coordinatorLayout"
    app:layout_anchorGravity="bottom|end|margin"/>
```

This button supports automatic styling, accessibility, and advanced animations.

10.2.3 Material Theming

Material Theming is a powerful feature in Material Design that allows you to customize the colors, typography, and shapes of your app's UI. You can define a custom theme in your res/values/themes.xml file and apply it across the entire app.

xml

```
<style name="AppTheme"
parent="Theme.MaterialComponents.DayNight.DarkActionBar">
    <item name="colorPrimary">@color/colorPrimary</item>
    <item name="colorPrimaryVariant">@color/colorPrimaryVariant</item>
    <item name="colorOnPrimary">@android:color/white</item>
    <item name="colorSecondary">@color/colorSecondary</item>
    <item name="colorOnSecondary">@android:color/black</item>
</style>
```

This makes it easier to apply a consistent look and feel across the app while ensuring accessibility and maintaining a responsive design.

10.3 Animations in Android: Making Your App Interactive with Smooth Transitions and Animations

10.3.1 Introduction to Animations

Animations enhance user interaction by providing feedback and guiding users through the app. Android offers a wide range of animation capabilities, from simple property animations (like changing a view's size or position) to complex transitions between activities or fragments.

The key to successful animations is ensuring they are smooth, subtle, and meaningful. Poorly designed animations can detract from the user experience, while well-crafted animations can improve usability, provide visual feedback, and add a layer of interactivity.

10.3.2 Types of Animations in Android

There are several types of animations you can use in Android, including:

- **View Animations**: Simple animations that manipulate the properties of a view (like position, size, rotation, or transparency).

- **Property Animations**: Advanced animations that can animate multiple properties of an object simultaneously.

- **Drawable Animations**: Animations that use frame-based animation (i.e., a sequence of images).

- **Transition Animations**: Animations between layout changes or transitions between activities/fragments.

10.3.3 View Animations

View animations are the simplest form of animation in Android. These animations use the Animation class and can manipulate a view's properties such as alpha, scale, rotation, and translation.

EXAMPLE OF A SIMPLE ANIMATION

Here's an example of animating the translation of a button across the screen:

kotlin

```kotlin
val button = findViewById<Button>(R.id.myButton)
val translateAnimation = TranslateAnimation(0f, 100f, 0f, 100f)
translateAnimation.duration = 1000  // 1-second animation
button.startAnimation(translateAnimation)
```

This will move the button from its original position to a new position over 1 second.

USING XML FOR VIEW ANIMATIONS

You can also define animations in XML under the res/anim/ directory. For example, here's an XML file that defines a fade-in animation:

xml

```xml
<!-- res/anim/fade_in.xml -->
<alpha xmlns:android="http://schemas.android.com/apk/res/android"
    android:duration="1000"
    android:fromAlpha="0.0"
    android:toAlpha="1.0"/>
```

To apply this animation in Kotlin:

kotlin

```kotlin
val fadeIn = AnimationUtils.loadAnimation(this, R.anim.fade_in)
view.startAnimation(fadeIn)
```

10.3.4 Property Animations

Property animations are more flexible and powerful than view animations. They can animate multiple properties of a view or object simultaneously, without relying on predefined XML animations.

OBJECTANIMATOR EXAMPLE

ObjectAnimator allows you to animate any property of an object. For example, animating a view's translation:

kotlin

```kotlin
val button = findViewById<Button>(R.id.myButton)
val animator = ObjectAnimator.ofFloat(button, "translationX", 0f, 300f)
animator.duration = 1000
animator.start()
```

This example animates the translationX property of the button from 0f to 300f over 1 second.

ANIMATORSET FOR MULTIPLE ANIMATIONS

You can use AnimatorSet to run multiple animations simultaneously or sequentially:

kotlin

```kotlin
val animator1 = ObjectAnimator.ofFloat(button, "translationX", 0f, 300f)
val animator2 = ObjectAnimator.ofFloat(button, "alpha", 1f, 0f)

val set = AnimatorSet()
set.playTogether(animator1, animator2)
set.duration = 1000
```

```
set.start()
```
This example animates both the position and the opacity of a button simultaneously.

10.3.5 Transition Animations

Transition animations allow for smooth transitions between different layouts or between activities/fragments. Android's **Transition API** enables animating changes in layout, view visibility, and fragment transactions.

BASIC TRANSITION EXAMPLE

kotlin

```
val transition = Fade()
transition.duration = 1000
TransitionManager.beginDelayedTransition(container, transition)
view.visibility = View.GONE
```
This will apply a fade transition to a view being hidden.

Conclusion

Mastering **Advanced UI Design** and **Animations** in Android is key to building visually appealing and highly interactive applications. **Custom Views and Widgets** provide the flexibility to create reusable, unique components that cater to the specific needs of your app. **Material Design** ensures that your app is not only aesthetically pleasing but also functional and consistent with modern design principles. Finally, **Animations** add polish and interactivity, ensuring a smooth and engaging user experience. By leveraging these techniques, you can create applications that not only look great but also feel responsive, intuitive, and enjoyable to use.

CHAPTER 11: HANDLING PERMISSIONS AND SYSTEM RESOURCES

In Android development, managing **permissions** and **system resources** is crucial for building efficient, secure, and user-friendly applications. Permissions in Android are required for accessing sensitive user data (such as location, camera, and storage), while system resources like battery, memory, and network connections must be optimized to ensure smooth performance and user satisfaction. Additionally, interacting with **external devices** like sensors, Bluetooth, and other hardware components adds another layer of complexity to app development.

This section provides a comprehensive guide to handling **permissions**, managing **system resources**, and working with **external devices** in Android. It will help you build apps that are secure, efficient, and capable of interacting with a wide range of devices and services.

11.1 Requesting Permissions: Handling Permissions for Camera, Location, Storage, and More

11.1.1 Understanding Permissions in Android

Permissions in Android are required for accessing sensitive resources on a user's device, such as the camera, location services, microphone, contacts, and storage. With Android's permission model, permissions are categorized into two types:

- **Normal Permissions**: These permissions are granted automatically when the app is installed. They do not affect the user's privacy or security. Examples include accessing the internet, setting the wallpaper, or reading the phone state.

- **Dangerous Permissions**: These permissions require explicit user consent because they grant access to sensitive data or features, such as the camera, location, or contacts. These permissions need to be requested at runtime.

Android 6.0 (API level 23) and higher introduced **runtime permissions**, meaning users must grant or deny permissions explicitly while the app is running, rather than during installation.

11.1.2 Defining Permissions in the AndroidManifest.xml

Permissions are defined in the AndroidManifest.xml file. For dangerous permissions, you must declare them in the manifest file to request the necessary access.

xml

```
<uses-permission android:name="android.permission.CAMERA"/>
<uses-permission
android:name="android.permission.ACCESS_FINE_LOCATION"/>
<uses-permission
android:name="android.permission.READ_EXTERNAL_STORAGE"/>
```

For normal permissions (e.g., internet access), you can define them as follows:

xml

```
<uses-permission android:name="android.permission.INTERNET"/>
```

11.1.3 Requesting Permissions at Runtime

For **dangerous permissions**, starting with Android 6.0 (API level 23), you must check whether the app has the required permission at runtime. If the app does not have the permission, you must request it from the user.

CHECKING FOR PERMISSIONS

Before requesting a permission, always check if it is already granted. This is done using the ContextCompat.checkSelfPermission() method.

kotlin

```kotlin
if (ContextCompat.checkSelfPermission(this, Manifest.permission.CAMERA)
!= PackageManager.PERMISSION_GRANTED) {
    // Permission not granted, request it
    ActivityCompat.requestPermissions(this,
arrayOf(Manifest.permission.CAMERA), CAMERA_REQUEST_CODE)
}
```

REQUESTING PERMISSIONS

To request permissions, use the requestPermissions() method. Here's how you can request camera permission:

kotlin

```kotlin
ActivityCompat.requestPermissions(this,
arrayOf(Manifest.permission.CAMERA), CAMERA_REQUEST_CODE)
```

This method will prompt the user with a dialog to allow or deny the permission. The result will be received in the onRequestPermissionsResult() method.

Handling Permission Request Results

After the user interacts with the permission request dialog, the result is handled in the onRequestPermissionsResult() method. The callback provides the permission status, allowing you to take appropriate action based on whether the user granted or denied the permission.

kotlin

```kotlin
override fun onRequestPermissionsResult(requestCode: Int, permissions:
Array<out String>, grantResults: IntArray) {
    when (requestCode) {
        CAMERA_REQUEST_CODE -> {
            if (grantResults.isNotEmpty() && grantResults[0] ==
PackageManager.PERMISSION_GRANTED) {
                // Permission granted, proceed with camera functionality
                openCamera()
            } else {
                // Permission denied, handle accordingly (e.g., show a message)
                Toast.makeText(this, "Camera permission denied",
Toast.LENGTH_SHORT).show()
            }
        }
    }
}
```

Explaining Why Permissions are Needed

For a better user experience, it's recommended to explain why certain permissions are required before requesting them. For example, if you need location access, it's good practice to show a dialog explaining the reason for the permission request.

kotlin

```kotlin
if (ActivityCompat.shouldShowRequestPermissionRationale(this,
Manifest.permission.ACCESS_FINE_LOCATION)) {
    // Show an explanation to the user why the permission is needed
```

```
Toast.makeText(this, "Location permission is required to access your current
location", Toast.LENGTH_SHORT).show()
} else {
    // Request the permission if rationale is not needed
    ActivityCompat.requestPermissions(this,
arrayOf(Manifest.permission.ACCESS_FINE_LOCATION),
LOCATION_REQUEST_CODE)
}
```

11.1.4 Common Permissions in Android

Let's look at a few commonly used permissions and how to request them in Android:

- **Camera Permission**: To access the camera, you must request CAMERA permission:

xml

```xml
<uses-permission android:name="android.permission.CAMERA"/>
```
Request it at runtime:

kotlin

```kotlin
if (ContextCompat.checkSelfPermission(this, Manifest.permission.CAMERA)
!= PackageManager.PERMISSION_GRANTED) {
    ActivityCompat.requestPermissions(this,
arrayOf(Manifest.permission.CAMERA), CAMERA_REQUEST_CODE)
}
```

- **Location Permission**: To access fine or coarse location data, request the ACCESS_FINE_LOCATION or ACCESS_COARSE_LOCATION permissions:

xml

```xml
<uses-permission
android:name="android.permission.ACCESS_FINE_LOCATION"/>
```
Request it at runtime:

kotlin

```
ActivityCompat.requestPermissions(this,
arrayOf(Manifest.permission.ACCESS_FINE_LOCATION),
LOCATION_REQUEST_CODE)
```

- **Storage Permission**: To read from or write to external storage, request the READ_EXTERNAL_STORAGE and WRITE_EXTERNAL_STORAGE permissions:

xml

```xml
<uses-permission
android:name="android.permission.READ_EXTERNAL_STORAGE"/>
<uses-permission
android:name="android.permission.WRITE_EXTERNAL_STORAGE"/>
```
Request it at runtime:

kotlin

```kotlin
ActivityCompat.requestPermissions(this,
arrayOf(Manifest.permission.READ_EXTERNAL_STORAGE),
STORAGE_REQUEST_CODE)
```

11.2 Managing System Resources: Optimizing Resource Usage (Battery, Memory, Network)

11.2.1 Battery Management in Android

Battery usage optimization is critical in mobile app development. Apps that drain the battery unnecessarily can lead to poor user experience and negative app reviews. Android provides several tools and best practices to manage and optimize battery usage.

EFFICIENT USE OF BACKGROUND SERVICES

Background services that perform periodic tasks (e.g., syncing data, monitoring location) can consume significant amounts of battery power. Android provides tools to minimize battery usage, such as **JobScheduler**, **WorkManager**, and **AlarmManager**.

- **JobScheduler**: For tasks that need to be scheduled at specific intervals.

- **WorkManager**: A robust API for scheduling background tasks that need to run even if the app is not actively running.

Here's an example of using **WorkManager** to handle background tasks:

kotlin

```
val workRequest = OneTimeWorkRequestBuilder<SyncWorker>()
    .setInitialDelay(1, TimeUnit.HOURS)
    .build()
```

```
WorkManager.getInstance(context).enqueue(workRequest)
```
This code schedules a task that runs every hour, reducing unnecessary battery consumption.

USING DOZE MODE AND APP STANDBY

In Android 6.0 (API level 23), **Doze mode** was introduced to optimize battery usage by reducing background tasks and network access when the device is not being used for an extended period. Make sure your app takes advantage of Doze mode to save battery when the device is idle.

kotlin

```
if (Build.VERSION.SDK_INT >= Build.VERSION_CODES.M) {
    val powerManager = getSystemService(Context.POWER_SERVICE) as
PowerManager
    if (powerManager.isDeviceIdleMode) {
        // Optimize task scheduling and background activities
    }
}
```

Reducing unnecessary network calls is another important factor in optimizing battery and resource usage. You can use **Caching**, **Request Throttling**, and **Compression** to reduce network overhead.

For example, Retrofit and OkHttp support caching HTTP responses:

kotlin

```
val cacheSize = 10 * 1024 * 1024 // 10 MB
val cache = Cache(applicationContext.cacheDir, cacheSize)

val okHttpClient = OkHttpClient.Builder()
  .cache(cache)
  .build()

val retrofit = Retrofit.Builder()
  .baseUrl("https://api.example.com")
  .client(okHttpClient)
  .build()
```

This helps prevent redundant network requests by using cached data, thus saving both battery and data usage.

11.3 Working with External Devices: Accessing Hardware Like Sensors and Bluetooth

11.3.1 Accessing Device Sensors

Android devices come with various sensors like the accelerometer, gyroscope, proximity sensor, and light sensor, which can be used to enhance the app's functionality. The SensorManager class allows developers to interact with these sensors and get real-time data.

WORKING WITH THE ACCELEROMETER

To access the accelerometer, you need to register a listener for sensor events:

kotlin

```kotlin
val sensorManager = getSystemService(Context.SENSOR_SERVICE) as
SensorManager
val accelerometer =
sensorManager.getDefaultSensor(Sensor.TYPE_ACCELEROMETER)

val sensorEventListener = object : SensorEventListener {
    override fun onSensorChanged(event: SensorEvent?) {
        if (event != null && event.sensor.type ==
Sensor.TYPE_ACCELEROMETER) {
            val x = event.values[0]
            val y = event.values[1]
            val z = event.values[2]
            // Use x, y, z for motion detection
        }
    }

    override fun onAccuracyChanged(sensor: Sensor?, accuracy: Int) {}
}

sensorManager.registerListener(sensorEventListener, accelerometer,
SensorManager.SENSOR_DELAY_UI)
```

This code listens for changes in the accelerometer's data and processes it in the onSensorChanged() method.

PROXIMITY SENSOR

The proximity sensor detects whether the device is near a user's face. This can be useful for features like turning off the screen during a phone call.

kotlin

```kotlin
val proximitySensor =
sensorManager.getDefaultSensor(Sensor.TYPE_PROXIMITY)
```

```kotlin
sensorManager.registerListener(object : SensorEventListener {
    override fun onSensorChanged(event: SensorEvent?) {
        if (event?.sensor?.type == Sensor.TYPE_PROXIMITY) {
            val distance = event.values[0]
            // Handle proximity sensor data
        }
    }

    override fun onAccuracyChanged(sensor: Sensor?, accuracy: Int) {}
}, proximitySensor, SensorManager.SENSOR_DELAY_UI)
```

11.3.2 Working with Bluetooth

Bluetooth is commonly used for connecting external devices like fitness trackers, wireless headphones, or smartwatches. To interact with Bluetooth devices, you need to request **Bluetooth** permissions in the AndroidManifest.xml:

xml

```xml
<uses-permission android:name="android.permission.BLUETOOTH"/>
<uses-permission
android:name="android.permission.BLUETOOTH_ADMIN"/>
<uses-permission
android:name="android.permission.ACCESS_FINE_LOCATION"/>
```

To enable Bluetooth and discover devices, use the BluetoothAdapter class:

kotlin

```kotlin
val bluetoothAdapter = BluetoothAdapter.getDefaultAdapter()

if (bluetoothAdapter == null) {
    // Device doesn't support Bluetooth
} else {
    if (!bluetoothAdapter.isEnabled) {
        val enableBtIntent =
Intent(BluetoothAdapter.ACTION_REQUEST_ENABLE)
        startActivityForResult(enableBtIntent, REQUEST_ENABLE_BT)
    }
}
```

To discover nearby Bluetooth devices:

kotlin

```
val discoverableIntent =
Intent(BluetoothAdapter.ACTION_REQUEST_DISCOVERABLE)
discoverableIntent.putExtra(BluetoothAdapter.EXTRA_DISCOVERABLE_DU
RATION, 300)
startActivity(discoverableIntent)
```

Once Bluetooth is enabled, you can connect to devices, transfer data, and interact with peripherals.

Conclusion

Handling permissions, managing system resources, and working with external devices are essential skills for any Android developer. By requesting permissions in a way that respects the user's privacy and optimizing the use of system resources, you can create apps that are both functional and efficient. Additionally, interacting with external devices like sensors and Bluetooth hardware expands the capabilities of your app, enabling you to build more complex and feature-rich mobile experiences. By following best practices for permissions, resource management, and hardware integration, you can ensure that your Android app performs well, remains secure, and provides a seamless user experience.

CHAPTER 12: TESTING AND DEBUGGING YOUR ANDROID APP

Testing and debugging are critical parts of the software development lifecycle. For Android app development, ensuring that your app functions as expected, performs well, and provides a seamless user experience is essential. Effective testing and debugging practices not only enhance the reliability and performance of the app but also save time and effort in the long run by catching bugs early.

In this comprehensive guide, we will explore **Unit Testing**, **UI Testing**, and **Debugging Tools** in Android. We'll discuss best practices for writing and executing tests, tools for debugging, and strategies for ensuring your app is reliable, user-friendly, and free from errors.

12.1 Unit Testing in Android: Writing Unit Tests to Ensure Your App's Reliability

12.1.1 What is Unit Testing?

Unit testing involves testing individual components or methods of an app in isolation to verify that they work correctly. In Android development, unit tests are typically written for the app's logic and non-UI components, such as methods in ViewModels, repositories, and other business logic components. Unit tests are essential for ensuring that your app's components behave as expected in different scenarios.

Unit tests are typically focused on:

- **Ensuring correctness**: Verifying that the app's methods return the correct results.

- **Test-driven development (TDD)**: Writing tests before implementing functionality to guide development.

- **Refactoring with confidence**: Ensuring that refactoring the code doesn't break existing functionality.

12.1.2 Writing Unit Tests in Android

In Android, **JUnit** is the most commonly used framework for writing unit tests. **JUnit 4** is included in Android projects by default, and with the introduction of **JUnit 5**, there are even more powerful features to streamline testing. However, when testing Android components, it's essential to separate out business logic from UI-related code, as UI testing falls under a different category.

SETTING UP JUNIT FOR UNIT TESTING

You need to add the following dependencies to your build.gradle file for unit testing with JUnit:

gradle

```
testImplementation 'junit:junit:4.13.2'
testImplementation 'org.mockito:mockito-core:3.9.0'  // For mocking objects
testImplementation 'androidx.arch.core:core-testing:2.1.0'  // For testing
LiveData
```

For **JUnit 5**, you can include the dependency:

gradle

```
testImplementation 'org.junit.jupiter:junit-jupiter-api:5.7.1'
testImplementation 'org.junit.jupiter:junit-jupiter-engine:5.7.1'
```

WRITING A SIMPLE UNIT TEST

Let's create a simple unit test for a method in a class that calculates the total price of items in a cart.

kotlin

```kotlin
class CartCalculator {

    fun calculateTotalPrice(cartItems: List<Item>): Double {
        return cartItems.sumByDouble { it.price }
    }
}

data class Item(val name: String, val price: Double)
```

Now, let's write a unit test to verify that the calculateTotalPrice method works correctly.

kotlin

```kotlin
class CartCalculatorTest {

    private lateinit var cartCalculator: CartCalculator

    @Before
    fun setup() {
        cartCalculator = CartCalculator()
    }

    @Test
    fun testCalculateTotalPrice() {
        val cartItems = listOf(
            Item("item1", 20.0),
            Item("item2", 30.0)
        )

        val total = cartCalculator.calculateTotalPrice(cartItems)

        assertEquals(50.0, total, 0.01)
    }
}
```

Here:

- @Before is used to initialize the class or setup the environment before each test runs.

- @Test defines the method that will be run as a unit test.

- assertEquals() checks whether the actual result matches the expected result, with a tolerance for floating-point calculations.

MOCKING DEPENDENCIES WITH MOCKITO

In unit tests, you may need to mock dependencies, such as services or network calls. Mockito is a popular mocking framework that helps with this.

For example, consider a class that retrieves data from an API:

kotlin

```kotlin
class ProductRepository(private val apiService: ApiService) {

    fun fetchProductDetails(productId: String): Product {
        return apiService.getProductDetails(productId)
    }
}
```
You can mock the ApiService dependency in your test like this:

kotlin

```kotlin
class ProductRepositoryTest {

    private lateinit var productRepository: ProductRepository
    private lateinit var apiService: ApiService

    @Before
    fun setup() {
        apiService = mock(ApiService::class.java)
        productRepository = ProductRepository(apiService)
    }
```

```
@Test
fun testFetchProductDetails() {
    val mockProduct = Product("product1", 100.0)

`when`(apiService.getProductDetails("product1")).thenReturn(mockProduct)

    val product = productRepository.fetchProductDetails("product1")

    assertEquals("product1", product.name)
    assertEquals(100.0, product.price, 0.01)
  }
}
```

- **Mockito's mock()** function creates a mock instance of the ApiService.

- **when()** is used to specify the behavior of the mock.

- **thenReturn()** defines what value the mock should return when called.

By using mocks, you ensure that unit tests focus on the logic of your components rather than external dependencies.

12.2 UI Testing: Using Espresso and UI Automator for Automated UI Testing

12.2.1 What is UI Testing?

UI testing involves testing the user interface components of the app to verify that they respond correctly to user actions and that the app behaves as expected in real-world scenarios. While unit tests focus on individual methods and business logic, UI tests ensure that users can interact with your app as intended. UI tests should verify that views are displayed correctly, buttons perform their actions, and transitions occur smoothly.

In Android, **Espresso** and **UI Automator** are two primary tools for automated UI testing.

12.2.2 Espresso: Automating UI Testing

Espresso is a testing framework provided by Google for testing Android UIs. It is widely used for writing concise and reliable tests for user interactions.

SETTING UP ESPRESSO

To set up Espresso for UI testing, add the following dependencies to your build.gradle file:

gradle

```
androidTestImplementation 'androidx.test.espresso:espresso-core:3.4.0'
androidTestImplementation 'androidx.test.ext:junit:1.1.3'
```

WRITING SIMPLE UI TESTS WITH ESPRESSO

Espresso allows you to simulate user actions like clicking buttons, entering text, or checking whether elements are visible on the screen.

For example, let's write a simple test to verify that a button performs the correct action when clicked.

1. **Activity under test:**

kotlin

```
class MainActivity : AppCompatActivity() {

    override fun onCreate(savedInstanceState: Bundle?) {
        super.onCreate(savedInstanceState)
        setContentView(R.layout.activity_main)
```

```kotlin
    val button = findViewById<Button>(R.id.myButton)
    button.setOnClickListener {
        findViewById<TextView>(R.id.myTextView).text = "Button Clicked!"
    }
  }
}
```

2. **Espresso test:**

kotlin

```kotlin
@RunWith(AndroidJUnit4::class)
class MainActivityTest {

    @Test
    fun testButtonClickUpdatesText() {
        // Launch the activity
        val activityScenario = ActivityScenario.launch(MainActivity::class.java)

        // Find the button and click it
        onView(withId(R.id.myButton)).perform(click())

        // Check if the text was updated
        onView(withId(R.id.myTextView)).check(matches(withText("Button
Clicked!")))
    }
}
```

In this example:

- onView(withId(R.id.myButton)) finds the button by its ID.

- perform(click()) simulates a click on the button.

- onView(withId(R.id.myTextView)) finds the TextView element.

- check(matches(withText("Button Clicked!"))) verifies that the text of the TextView was updated after the button click.

Espresso provides methods to simulate almost every interaction in the app, including typing in text fields, scrolling through lists, and checking visibility of views.

Handling Asynchronous Operations

Espresso automatically synchronizes with the UI thread and waits for animations or background tasks to finish before continuing the test. However, sometimes you may need to explicitly wait for a background operation, such as a network request. You can use IdlingResource to wait for asynchronous operations to complete.

kotlin

```
val idlingResource = MyIdlingResource()
Espresso.registerIdlingResources(idlingResource)
```
This ensures that Espresso will wait for the background operation to finish before continuing with the next assertion.

12.2.3 UI Automator: Testing Across Apps and Device Interactions

While **Espresso** is great for testing interactions within a single app, **UI Automator** is designed to test interactions across different apps and the device itself. For example, UI Automator can be used to simulate interaction with the system settings, other apps, or device notifications.

Setting Up UI Automator

Add the following dependencies to use UI Automator:

gradle

```
androidTestImplementation 'androidx.test.uiautomator:uiautomator:2.2.0'
```

Writing UI Automator Tests

Here's an example of using UI Automator to check if the "Wi-Fi" option in the Android settings is visible:

```kotlin
@RunWith(AndroidJUnit4::class)
class SettingsTest {

    @Test
    fun testWiFiOption() {
        val device =
UiDevice.getInstance(InstrumentationRegistry.getInstrumentation())
        device.pressHome()

        val allAppsButton = device.findObject(UiSelector().description("Apps"))
        allAppsButton.click()

        val settingsApp = device.findObject(UiSelector().text("Settings"))
        settingsApp.click()

        val wifiOption = device.findObject(UiSelector().text("Wi-Fi"))
        assertTrue(wifiOption.exists())
    }
}
```

In this example:

- UiDevice.getInstance() gets the current device instance.

- UiSelector() is used to find UI elements by their properties (like text, description).

- assertTrue() checks if the "Wi-Fi" option exists.

UI Automator can also handle notifications, interacting with multiple apps, and performing system-level interactions that Espresso cannot handle.

12.3 Debugging Tools: Leveraging Android Studio's Built-in Tools for Effective Debugging

12.3.1 Debugging in Android Studio

Debugging is an essential part of the development process. Android Studio provides powerful debugging tools to help developers identify and fix bugs in their code. These tools include breakpoints, step-through debugging, logcat, and memory analysis tools.

SETTING BREAKPOINTS

Breakpoints allow you to pause the execution of your app at specific lines of code. You can then inspect the state of variables, step through the code line by line, and identify issues.

To set a breakpoint:

1. Open the Kotlin file you want to debug.

2. Click the gutter next to the line number where you want to pause the app. A red dot will appear.

3. Run the app in debug mode (Shift + F9), and the execution will stop at the breakpoint.

While debugging, you can inspect the **Variables** and **Watches** panels to view the current values of variables, and use the **Call Stack** panel to view the current execution stack.

STEP THROUGH CODE

Once a breakpoint is hit, you can step through the code using the following options:

- **Step Over (F8)**: Execute the current line of code and move to the next one.

- **Step Into (F7)**: Dive into the method or function call to see its details.

- **Step Out (Shift + F8)**: Exit the current method and return to the calling method.

LOGCAT FOR LOGGING

Logcat is a powerful logging system in Android Studio that provides real-time logs for your app. It allows you to track system logs, debug messages, warnings, and errors.

Use Log.d(), Log.i(), Log.e(), and other methods to print logs for different purposes:

kotlin

```
Log.d("MainActivity", "This is a debug message")
```
You can filter logs in Logcat based on severity (debug, info, error), tag, or app process. This helps you quickly isolate issues.

Conclusion

Testing and debugging are fundamental practices that ensure the reliability, stability, and performance of your Android app. Unit testing verifies the functionality of individual components, UI testing with Espresso and UI Automator ensures your app's user interface works seamlessly, and Android Studio's built-in debugging tools make it easy to identify and fix issues. By incorporating these practices into your development workflow, you can create high-quality Android apps that perform as expected and provide users with an excellent experience.

CHAPTER 12: OPTIMIZING APP PERFORMANCE

In Android development, performance optimization is crucial for delivering an exceptional user experience. A sluggish app not only frustrates users but can lead to poor reviews, high uninstall rates, and ultimately, reduced user retention. Optimizing app performance involves addressing various factors that impact speed, responsiveness, and resource consumption, such as memory management, CPU usage, network requests, and UI responsiveness.

In this guide, we will explore **Memory Management**, **Profiling Your App**, and strategies for **Speeding Up Your App** to ensure that your app performs optimally across different devices and network conditions.

13.1 Memory Management: Avoiding Memory Leaks and Optimizing Memory Usage

13.1.1 Understanding Memory Management in Android

Memory management is one of the most critical aspects of app performance. Improper memory usage can lead to slow performance, crashes, and even app termination by the Android operating system due to excessive memory consumption. Android provides a **garbage collector** that automatically manages memory for most objects, but developers still need to be mindful of memory leaks and optimize memory usage.

In Android, memory management primarily involves:

- **Allocating memory efficiently**: Allocating memory for objects and resources only when needed.

- **Avoiding memory leaks**: Ensuring that objects are properly cleaned up when they are no longer needed.

- **Reducing memory footprint**: Using resources like images, databases, and assets in a memory-efficient way.

13.1.2 Memory Leaks and How to Avoid Them

A **memory leak** occurs when objects are no longer needed but are still being referenced, preventing the garbage collector from reclaiming that memory. Common causes of memory leaks in Android include:

- **Holding references to context objects** (e.g., Activity or View) after they are no longer needed.

- **Not unregistering listeners** or observers (e.g., BroadcastReceiver, SensorEventListener).

- **Improper use of static fields**: Static references that hold onto objects, such as Views or Context, can leak memory.

COMMON SCENARIOS FOR MEMORY LEAKS

1. **Activity or Fragment Context Leaks**

Avoid holding a reference to the Activity or Context object in a long-lived object (such as a static field or background thread), as this will prevent the Activity from being garbage collected when it is destroyed.

kotlin

```kotlin
// WRONG: Holding a reference to Activity context
val someObject = object : Runnable {
    override fun run() {
        val context = activityContext // Activity context reference
        // Some background operation
    }
}
```

Instead, use WeakReference for long-lived references to Activity or Context:

kotlin

```kotlin
val contextRef = WeakReference(activityContext)
```

2. Listener and Observer Leaks

If you register listeners or observers (like BroadcastReceiver, SensorEventListener, OnClickListener), make sure to unregister them when they are no longer needed.

kotlin

```kotlin
// WRONG: Forgetting to unregister listener
override fun onResume() {
    super.onResume()
    sensorManager.registerListener(sensorEventListener, sensor,
SensorManager.SENSOR_DELAY_UI)
}

override fun onPause() {
    super.onPause()
    // Should unregister the listener to avoid memory leaks
    sensorManager.unregisterListener(sensorEventListener)
}
```

3. Static Field Leaks

Avoid holding references to Activity or Context in static fields, as this will prevent the Activity from being garbage collected:

kotlin

```
// WRONG: Static reference to Activity context
companion object {
    var contextRef: Context? = null
}
```

USING LEAKCANARY FOR DETECTING MEMORY LEAKS

LeakCanary is an open-source library that helps you detect memory leaks in Android apps. It automatically detects leaks and provides detailed information about the cause.

To integrate LeakCanary:

1. Add the dependency to your build.gradle file:

gradle

```
debugImplementation 'com.squareup.leakcanary:leakcanary-android:2.7'
```

2. LeakCanary will automatically detect and notify you about memory leaks during development, allowing you to fix them before releasing the app.

13.1.3 Optimizing Memory Usage

Efficient memory usage involves minimizing the memory footprint of objects and resources within the app. Here are a few key strategies:

1. **Efficient Image Handling**

Images can take up a significant amount of memory, especially in apps with lots of media. Use the following practices to handle images efficiently:

- **Use BitmapFactory for Efficient Image Loading**: Avoid loading large images into memory if they aren't necessary. Use BitmapFactory to load scaled-down versions of images.

kotlin

```
val options = BitmapFactory.Options()
options.inSampleSize = 2 // Load an image at half its size
val bitmap = BitmapFactory.decodeResource(resources, R.drawable.image, options)
```

- **Use Glide or Picasso for Image Loading**: These libraries automatically handle memory-efficient image loading, caching, and resizing.

2. Using SparseArrays Instead of HashMaps

For storing mappings between integers and objects, SparseArray can be more memory-efficient than HashMap, especially when the number of items is small.

kotlin

```
val sparseArray = SparseArray<String>()
sparseArray.put(1, "One")
sparseArray.put(2, "Two")
```

3. Optimizing Bitmaps with Bitmap.recycle()

Once you are done using a Bitmap object, explicitly call recycle() to release the memory associated with it.

kotlin

```
bitmap.recycle()
```

13.1.4 Managing Large Data Sets Efficiently

When working with large data sets, such as JSON responses or database records, be mindful of memory consumption. Consider using **paging** or **streaming** techniques to load data in chunks instead of all at once, which can reduce memory overhead.

For example, with the **Paging** library, you can load data from the network or database in small chunks, reducing memory usage and improving app performance:

gradle

implementation "androidx.paging:paging-runtime:3.0.0"

13.2 Profiling Your App: Using Android Studio's Profiler Tools to Improve App Performance

13.2.1 Introduction to Android Profiler

Android Studio provides a set of **profiler tools** that allow you to monitor your app's performance in real time. The **Android Profiler** helps you track critical performance metrics, such as CPU usage, memory usage, network activity, and battery consumption. By profiling your app, you can identify performance bottlenecks and optimize resource usage.

The Android Profiler provides the following tools:

1. **CPU Profiler**: Monitors your app's CPU usage, helping you identify performance bottlenecks caused by excessive CPU consumption.

2. **Memory Profiler**: Tracks memory usage and helps you identify memory leaks, inefficient memory allocation, or high memory consumption.

3. **Network Profiler**: Monitors network requests and helps optimize network usage, including identifying slow requests or large payloads.

4. **Energy Profiler**: Helps you identify which parts of your app are consuming too much battery.

13.2.2 Using the CPU Profiler

The CPU Profiler helps you analyze how your app is utilizing the device's CPU, which is essential for optimizing performance and reducing battery consumption.

RECORDING CPU ACTIVITY

To start profiling your app's CPU usage:

1. Open **Android Studio** and navigate to **View > Tool Windows > Profiler**.

2. Select your device and app from the list.

3. Choose the **CPU Profiler** tab.

4. Click the **Record** button to start recording CPU activity while interacting with your app.

The CPU Profiler displays a timeline of CPU activity, including **method traces** and **threads**. You can drill down into specific methods to identify which parts of your code are consuming the most CPU time.

13.2.3 Using the Memory Profiler

The **Memory Profiler** tracks memory usage and helps you identify objects that consume too much memory or are not being garbage collected. It allows you to monitor the memory usage of your app in real-time and take snapshots of the heap.

Tracking Memory Usage

To profile memory usage:

1. Open the **Memory Profiler** in Android Studio.

2. Click the **Record** button to start tracking memory usage.

3. Use your app and observe how memory usage increases.

4. You can also take a **Heap Dump** to see what objects are occupying memory.

The Memory Profiler shows memory allocations, including instances of each object and their reference chains. By analyzing this data, you can identify memory leaks and unnecessary memory usage.

13.2.4 Using the Network Profiler

The **Network Profiler** helps you monitor network activity, including data sent and received by your app. It is essential for optimizing network requests, reducing data usage, and improving app responsiveness.

Tracking Network Requests

To profile network usage:

1. Open the **Network Profiler** tab in Android Studio.

2. Click the **Record** button to start tracking network requests.

3. Interact with your app to generate network activity.

The Network Profiler will show all network requests, including the URL, response time, data sent and received, and the status of each request. By analyzing this data, you can identify slow network requests and large payloads that could be optimized.

13.3 Speeding Up Your App: Optimizing Network Requests, UI Responsiveness, and Load Times

13.3.1 Optimizing Network Requests

Network requests are often one of the biggest performance bottlenecks in mobile apps. Optimizing network calls can reduce latency, save battery life, and improve the overall user experience. Here are a few strategies to optimize network requests:

1. REDUCE THE NUMBER OF NETWORK REQUESTS

Minimize the number of network requests by batching requests or using **caching**. For example, if your app needs to fetch data from multiple endpoints, consider using **GraphQL** to consolidate multiple requests into a single query.

2. USE CACHING TO AVOID REDUNDANT REQUESTS

Caching network responses locally can drastically improve the performance of your app, especially when users are offline or have limited connectivity. Both Retrofit and OkHttp support response caching out-of-the-box:

kotlin

```kotlin
val cache = Cache(application.cacheDir, 10 * 1024 * 1024)  // 10 MB
val client = OkHttpClient.Builder().cache(cache).build()
```

3. COMPRESS DATA TO REDUCE PAYLOAD SIZE

Reduce the size of the data being transferred by compressing responses. You can use **Gzip** compression to compress the response body on the server and decompress it on the client side.

kotlin

```kotlin
val request = Request.Builder()
    .url(url)
    .header("Accept-Encoding", "gzip")
    .build()
```

4. OPTIMIZE REQUEST AND RESPONSE HANDLING

Avoid blocking the main thread with network requests. Use **asynchronous** network calls to ensure that the app remains responsive:

kotlin

```kotlin
val call = retrofitService.getData()
call.enqueue(object : Callback<ResponseData> {
    override fun onResponse(call: Call<ResponseData>, response:
Response<ResponseData>) {
        // Handle the response
    }

    override fun onFailure(call: Call<ResponseData>, t: Throwable) {
        // Handle failure
    }
})
```

13.3.2 Improving UI Responsiveness

The UI is the part of the app that users interact with most frequently. Ensuring smooth UI interactions is key to providing a good user experience. The following tips can help you improve UI responsiveness:

1. AVOID LONG OPERATIONS ON THE MAIN THREAD

Performing heavy operations, such as network requests or database queries, on the main thread can cause the UI to freeze or become unresponsive. Offload these operations to background threads using **AsyncTask, Handler,** or **Kotlin Coroutines**.

kotlin

```kotlin
GlobalScope.launch(Dispatchers.IO) {
    val result = networkCall() // Background work
    withContext(Dispatchers.Main) {
        updateUI(result) // Update the UI on the main thread
    }
}
```

2. USE EFFICIENT LAYOUTS

Nested layouts, especially deep hierarchy trees, can slow down the rendering process. Use **ConstraintLayout** or **LinearLayout** instead of deeply nested RelativeLayout or FrameLayout hierarchies to improve layout performance.

3. USE GPU-ACCELERATED VIEWS

For complex animations or custom views, make sure to use hardware acceleration, which offloads rendering tasks to the device's GPU, improving performance. You can enable hardware acceleration in the app's manifest:

xml

<application android:hardwareAccelerated="true" />

4. OPTIMIZE LIST VIEWS

For apps displaying large data sets, use **RecyclerView** with **ViewHolder** to avoid creating and binding views unnecessarily. RecyclerView only creates views for the items currently on screen, improving performance in scrolling lists.

13.3.3 Reducing Load Times

Long load times are one of the most frustrating issues for users. Minimizing app load times is essential for providing a smooth user experience.

1. USE SPLASH SCREENS WISELY

Splash screens are often used to display branding or perform initial setup, but they can also delay the user from interacting with the app. Minimize the duration of the splash screen and ensure that any heavy work (such as network requests or database queries) is done in the background.

2. OPTIMIZE DATABASE QUERIES

Ensure that database queries are optimized by:

- Using **indexes** for frequently queried columns.

- Avoiding **N+1 query problems** by preloading related data in a single query.

3. LOAD DATA ON DEMAND

Instead of loading all data at once, implement **lazy loading** to fetch only what is necessary. For example, load images and data as the user scrolls through a list.

Conclusion

Optimizing app performance is a continuous process that involves addressing various aspects, including **memory management**, **network requests**, **UI responsiveness**, and **load times**. By following the best practices outlined in this guide, you can ensure that your Android app runs efficiently, consumes minimal resources, and provides a smooth, responsive experience for users. Proper testing, profiling, and optimization will not only improve the performance of your app but also enhance user retention and satisfaction.

CHAPTER 14: DEPLOYING AND PUBLISHING YOUR APP

Building a great Android app is only half of the journey. To ensure that your app reaches your target audience, performs well on their devices, and generates revenue, you must go through a careful deployment and publishing process. This process involves preparing your app for release, publishing it to the **Google Play Store**, and implementing effective **marketing** and **monetization** strategies. Proper deployment and publication can lead to a successful launch and long-term app growth.

In this comprehensive guide, we'll cover everything you need to know about **preparing your app for release**, **publishing to the Google Play Store**, and **marketing and monetizing** your app. Each of these steps is crucial to ensuring your app's success in the competitive app market.

14.1 Preparing Your App for Release: Creating Signed APKs and App Bundles

Before you can publish your Android app to the **Google Play Store**, you need to prepare it for release. This involves creating a signed APK or app bundle, which is a binary file that can be installed on users' devices. Google Play requires apps to be signed with a secure key to verify the authenticity of the developer and ensure the integrity of the app.

14.1.1 Understanding APK and App Bundles

- **APK (Android Package)**: APK files are the traditional format for distributing and installing Android apps. They contain all the resources, code, and assets needed for the app to run. APKs are directly installed on the device.

- **App Bundle (AAB - Android App Bundle)**: The Android App Bundle is a newer, more efficient format introduced by Google. App Bundles allow for **dynamic delivery**, which means that Google Play can generate optimized APKs for different device configurations (e.g., screen sizes, CPU architectures) from a single app bundle. App Bundles are recommended for new apps and are required if you want to use features like **Play Feature Delivery** and **Play Asset Delivery**.

The key difference between the two formats is that an APK is a complete installation package, while an app bundle is a format that allows Google Play to generate APKs dynamically based on the user's device specifications.

14.1.2 Creating a Signed APK or App Bundle

To distribute your app securely and ensure it's trusted by Google Play, you must sign it with a digital certificate. Here's how you can do this in Android Studio:

STEP 1: GENERATE A KEYSTORE FILE

A keystore is a file containing private keys used to sign your app. It's essential for securing your app and ensuring its integrity. To generate a keystore file:

1. Open **Android Studio**.

2. Navigate to **Build > Generate Signed Bundle / APK**.

3. Choose either **APK** or **Android App Bundle (AAB)** depending on your preference.

4. Select **Create New** to generate a new keystore file.

5. Enter the necessary information:

   - **Key store path**: Location where the keystore file will be stored.

   - **Key alias**: A name for your key.

   - **Key password**: A password for your key.

   - **Key validity (years)**: Set the validity period for the key.

   - **Your name** and **organization information**.

Once the keystore file is generated, it will be used to sign your APK or app bundle.

STEP 2: SIGNING THE APK OR APP BUNDLE

1. After creating the keystore, go back to the **Generate Signed Bundle / APK** dialog in Android Studio.

2. Select **APK** or **Android App Bundle**.

3. Choose **Release** as the build variant.

4. Under **Key store**, browse and select the keystore file you just created.

5. Enter the **Key alias** and **Key password**.

6. Once everything is set, click **Finish**.

Android Studio will then generate a signed APK or app bundle. If you're generating an APK, it will be ready to distribute. If you're generating an app bundle, Android Studio will create an .aab file, which will be used to publish your app on the Play Store.

14.1.3 Testing Your Signed APK or App Bundle

Before uploading your signed APK or app bundle to the Google Play Store, it's essential to test it thoroughly. Use the following methods to ensure that your app is ready for release:

- **Install the APK on a physical device**: Transfer the signed APK to a physical device to test if the app runs smoothly and behaves as expected.

- **Test with different configurations**: If you're using an app bundle, test the app on various devices (e.g., different screen sizes and resolutions, various Android versions) to ensure compatibility.

- **Check for crashes and errors**: Use **Logcat** to monitor the app's behavior and identify any potential crashes or errors during testing.

14.2 Publishing to the Google Play Store: Step-by-Step Guide to Submitting Your App

Once your app is ready for release, the next step is to submit it to the **Google Play Store**. This involves creating a developer account, filling out necessary app details, uploading your app bundle or APK, and setting up monetization (if applicable).

14.2.1 Creating a Google Play Developer Account

To publish an app on the Google Play Store, you need to create a **Google Play Developer account**:

1. Go to the Google Play Console and sign in with your Google account.

2. Pay the **one-time registration fee** of $25 (USD).

3. Follow the instructions to complete the registration process. You'll need to provide some personal information, including a developer name, email address, and website (optional).

Once your developer account is set up, you can start uploading your apps to the Google Play Store.

14.2.2 Preparing App Store Listing Information

Before submitting your app, you must prepare the following information to create your app's store listing:

- **App name**: A unique name for your app that appears on the Play Store.

- **Short description**: A brief summary of your app's functionality (under 80 characters).

- **Full description**: A detailed description that explains what your app does, how it works, and its unique features.

- **Screenshots**: Screenshots of your app that show its key features. You'll need to upload screenshots for different device types (e.g., phone, tablet).

- **App icon**: A high-resolution icon that represents your app. The icon should be 512 x 512 pixels and less than 1024 KB in size.

- **Feature graphic**: A banner image that will appear at the top of your app's Play Store listing. The size should be 1024 x 500 pixels.

- **Category**: Select a category that best describes your app (e.g., Productivity, Games, Social).

- **Privacy policy**: If your app collects sensitive user data (e.g., location, contacts), you'll need to provide a privacy policy URL.

- **Content rating**: Answer questions about the content of your app (e.g., age suitability).

- **Target audience**: Select the audience you're targeting (e.g., everyone, children).

14.2.3 Uploading Your App Bundle or APK

Once your app listing is ready, you can upload the signed APK or app bundle to the Google Play Console:

1. In the Google Play Console, go to the **"Release"** section and select **"Production"**.

2. Click on **"Create Release"**.

3. Upload your APK or app bundle.

4. Google Play Console will check your app for any issues and display a list of warnings or errors (if any).

5. If everything looks good, click **"Save"** to finalize your release.

14.2.4 Setting Up Pricing and Distribution

After uploading your app, you'll need to configure the pricing and distribution settings:

- **Pricing**: Decide whether your app will be free or paid. Keep in mind that Google Play takes a percentage of sales from paid apps and in-app purchases (usually 30%).

- **Countries and regions**: Select which countries your app will be available in.

- **Devices and features**: Choose which devices your app supports (e.g., phones, tablets, wearables). You can also configure compatibility with specific Android versions and screen sizes.

14.2.5 Publishing Your App

Once all information is complete, click **"Review"** to ensure everything is correct, and then hit **"Publish"**. After submission, it will take anywhere from a few hours to a few days for Google to review and approve your app.

- **Approval process**: Google will review your app for compliance with its policies (e.g., content, security). If approved, your app will be available for download on the Google Play Store.

14.3 Marketing and Monetizing Your App:

14.3.1 Marketing Your App

Marketing your app is essential to getting it noticed in the competitive app market. A strong marketing strategy can help you reach a wider audience, drive installations, and engage users. Here are some strategies for marketing your app:

1. APP STORE OPTIMIZATION (ASO)

App Store Optimization (ASO) is the process of optimizing your app's listing on the Google Play Store to increase its visibility and downloads. ASO involves optimizing the following:

- **App title**: Include relevant keywords in your app's title to improve search visibility.

- **Description**: Write a clear and concise description with targeted keywords. Ensure that it highlights your app's unique features and benefits.

- **Keywords**: Research the best keywords related to your app and include them in the description, title, and tags.

- **Screenshots and videos**: Showcase your app's key features with high-quality screenshots and demo videos.

- **Ratings and reviews**: Encourage users to leave positive ratings and reviews. Responding to reviews can also help improve your app's credibility.

2. SOCIAL MEDIA MARKETING

Leverage social media platforms like Facebook, Instagram, Twitter, and LinkedIn to promote your app. You can run paid ads or post content related to your app to engage potential users.

- **Create engaging posts**: Post about new features, updates, and special offers. Share user testimonials and app success stories.

- **Influencer marketing**: Partner with influencers to reach a broader audience and gain credibility.

- **Referral programs**: Offer users incentives (e.g., free features or premium access) for referring friends to your app.

3. CONTENT MARKETING AND SEO

Content marketing involves creating and distributing valuable content to attract and engage users. Start a blog, write articles about topics related to your app, and optimize your content for search engines (SEO) to drive organic traffic.

4. PAID ADVERTISING

Paid advertising is another way to reach potential users quickly. Use Google Ads, Facebook Ads, and other ad platforms to run targeted campaigns that bring traffic to your app's Play Store listing.

- **Google Ads**: Create app-install campaigns that target users who are likely to download your app based on demographics, interests, or behavior.

- **Facebook Ads**: Run app-install ads or promote content that encourages users to download the app.

14.3.2 Monetizing Your App

Once your app is available, it's time to start earning revenue. There are several monetization strategies to choose from, depending on your app's type, target audience, and goals.

1. IN-APP ADVERTISING

In-app advertising is one of the most common ways to monetize apps. Ads are displayed within the app, and you earn money based on ad impressions, clicks, or conversions. You can use ad networks like **Google AdMob**, **Facebook Audience Network**, or **Unity Ads** to display ads.

- **Banner ads**: Small, static ads displayed at the top or bottom of the screen.

- **Interstitial ads**: Full-screen ads that appear during natural app transitions (e.g., between levels in a game).

- **Rewarded ads**: Ads that provide users with rewards (e.g., in-game currency) for watching ads.

2. IN-APP PURCHASES

In-app purchases (IAP) allow you to sell virtual goods, subscriptions, or premium content directly within your app. This is a popular model for gaming apps and apps with recurring content.

- **Consumable items**: Items that are used once (e.g., virtual currency).

- **Non-consumable items**: Items that users buy once and own forever (e.g., premium features).

- **Subscriptions**: Recurring payments for ongoing access to content or features (e.g., monthly or yearly subscriptions).

3. Paid Apps

If your app offers significant value or unique functionality, you can charge users to download it. This is typically used for apps that provide specialized tools, professional services, or premium content.

4. Sponsorship and Partnerships

If your app gains a significant user base, you can partner with brands to offer sponsored content or co-branded experiences. This model works well for apps with niche audiences.

Conclusion

Deploying and publishing your Android app is a multi-step process that involves preparing your app for release, submitting it to the Google Play Store, and employing effective marketing and monetization strategies. By following the steps outlined in this guide, you can successfully navigate the complexities of app publishing, maximize your app's visibility, and generate revenue through various monetization methods. Keep in mind that marketing and monetization require continuous effort and iteration, but with the right strategy, your app can thrive in the competitive app market.

CHAPTER 15: EXPLORING ADVANCED TOPICS AND NEXT STEPS

As an Android developer, it's crucial to continually expand your knowledge and skills to keep up with the ever-evolving landscape of mobile development. Whether you're building enterprise-level applications or innovative startups, mastering advanced concepts and tools is key to crafting high-quality, maintainable apps. In this comprehensive guide, we'll explore three important topics for advanced Android development:

1. **Jetpack Libraries**: Understanding Android's modern libraries for building robust apps.

2. **Android Architecture Components**: Using ViewModel, LiveData, and other architecture components to create scalable, maintainable apps.

3. **Career Development in Android Development**: Identifying opportunities for career growth, certifications, and resources for continued learning.

These topics will not only enhance your app development skills but also help you navigate your career path as an Android developer.

15.1 Jetpack Libraries: Exploring Android's Modern Libraries for Building Robust Apps

15.1.1 What is Jetpack?

Jetpack is a suite of modern, open-source libraries designed to help developers write high-quality apps more easily and quickly. It provides tools for handling tasks like UI, navigation, and lifecycle management, as well as for managing data and accessing system services. Jetpack libraries offer best practices, reducing boilerplate code and making your apps more maintainable and scalable.

Jetpack consists of a set of libraries grouped into different categories, including:

- **Architecture**: Components for managing UI and data efficiently.

- **UI**: Components for building user interfaces with ease.

- **Behavior**: Tools for handling device capabilities and system features.

- **Foundation**: Fundamental libraries for app development.

Jetpack is fully backward compatible, meaning that these libraries can be used with older Android versions, ensuring that your app runs smoothly across a wide range of devices.

15.1.2 Key Jetpack Libraries for Modern App Development

Below are some of the most important Jetpack libraries that can help you build robust, scalable apps:

1. NAVIGATION COMPONENT

The **Navigation Component** helps you implement a robust and scalable navigation pattern within your app. It simplifies the process of managing fragments, activities, and navigation actions, ensuring that you follow best practices for navigation within your app. It provides a single activity, single fragment architecture with deep linking, up and back actions, and navigation graph handling.

Example of setting up navigation:

xml

```xml
<fragment
    android:id="@+id/firstFragment"
    android:name="com.example.app.FirstFragment"
    android:label="First Fragment"
    tools:layout="@layout/fragment_first" />
```
And handling navigation in your activity:

kotlin

```kotlin
val navController = findNavController(R.id.nav_host_fragment)
navController.navigate(R.id.action_firstFragment_to_secondFragment)
```

2. LIVEDATA

LiveData is an observable data holder that helps you manage UI-related data in a lifecycle-conscious manner. It ensures that your UI components only receive updates when they are in an active state (e.g., when they are in the foreground). LiveData works well with **ViewModel**, allowing your app to survive configuration changes like screen rotations.

Example:

kotlin

```kotlin
class MyViewModel : ViewModel() {
```

```kotlin
    private val _liveData = MutableLiveData<String>()
    val liveData: LiveData<String> get() = _liveData

    fun updateData(newData: String) {
        _liveData.value = newData
    }
}
```

3. VIEWMODEL

ViewModel is designed to store and manage UI-related data in a way that survives configuration changes. ViewModel separates UI-related data from UI controllers like activities and fragments, allowing your app to maintain UI consistency even after screen rotations.

Example:

kotlin

```kotlin
class MyViewModel : ViewModel() {
    private val data = MutableLiveData<String>()

    fun getData(): LiveData<String> = data

    fun updateData(newData: String) {
        data.value = newData
    }
}
```

In your activity or fragment:

kotlin

```kotlin
val viewModel = ViewModelProvider(this).get(MyViewModel::class.java)
viewModel.getData().observe(viewLifecycleOwner, Observer { data ->
    // Update UI with the new data
})
```

4. ROOM DATABASE

Room is an abstraction layer over SQLite that simplifies database operations and reduces boilerplate code. It allows you to access your app's database using a simple API. Room supports LiveData, enabling you to observe changes to database data in real-time.

Example of setting up a Room database:

```kotlin
@Entity(tableName = "user_table")
data class User(
    @PrimaryKey(autoGenerate = true) val id: Int,
    val name: String,
    val age: Int
)

@Dao
interface UserDao {
    @Insert
    suspend fun insert(user: User)

    @Query("SELECT * FROM user_table")
    fun getAllUsers(): LiveData<List<User>>
}

@Database(entities = [User::class], version = 1)
abstract class UserDatabase : RoomDatabase() {
    abstract fun userDao(): UserDao
}
```

5. WORKMANAGER

WorkManager is a library that simplifies background task management, particularly for tasks that need to be executed even if the app is closed or the device is rebooted. WorkManager helps you schedule tasks such as network requests, data sync, or file uploads, ensuring that they run reliably.

Example:

kotlin

```
val workRequest = OneTimeWorkRequestBuilder<MyWorker>()
    .setInitialDelay(1, TimeUnit.HOURS)
    .build()

WorkManager.getInstance(context).enqueue(workRequest)
```

6. DATA BINDING

Data Binding enables you to bind UI components to data sources in a declarative way. It reduces the need for findViewById() calls and makes your code more concise and readable.

Example:

xml

```xml
<TextView
    android:id="@+id/textView"
    android:layout_width="wrap_content"
    android:layout_height="wrap_content"
    android:text="@{viewModel.userName}" />
```

In the ViewModel:

kotlin

```kotlin
class MyViewModel : ViewModel() {
    val userName = MutableLiveData<String>()
}
```

By leveraging Jetpack libraries, Android developers can write cleaner, more maintainable code and ensure that their apps follow best practices for architecture, UI design, and background processing.

15.2 Android Architecture Components: Using ViewModel, LiveData, and Other Architecture Components

15.2.1 Introduction to Android Architecture Components

Android Architecture Components are a set of libraries designed to help developers design robust, maintainable, and testable apps. These components are based on modern Android development best practices, including **MVVM** (Model-View-ViewModel) and **MVP** (Model-View-Presenter) patterns.

The core components of Android architecture are:

- **ViewModel**: Stores and manages UI-related data.

- **LiveData**: A lifecycle-aware data holder that allows UI components to observe data changes.

- **Room**: A persistence library for managing local databases.

- **WorkManager**: Manages background tasks.

- **Lifecycle**: Provides lifecycle-aware components for activities and fragments.

- **Navigation**: Handles navigation between different parts of the app.

These components are designed to work together to create scalable, modular, and maintainable Android apps.

15.2.2 ViewModel and LiveData in Action

The **ViewModel** component is used to store and manage UI-related data that survives configuration changes. **LiveData** is an observable data holder, often used in conjunction with ViewModel, to provide data to UI components like activities and fragments.

Here's how to implement **ViewModel** and **LiveData** in your app:

1. **Create the ViewModel:**

kotlin

```kotlin
class MainViewModel : ViewModel() {
   private val _userName = MutableLiveData<String>()
   val userName: LiveData<String> get() = _userName

   fun fetchUserData() {
      _userName.value = "John Doe"
   }
}
```

2. **Observe the LiveData** in the Activity or Fragment:

kotlin

```kotlin
class MainActivity : AppCompatActivity() {

   private lateinit var mainViewModel: MainViewModel

   override fun onCreate(savedInstanceState: Bundle?) {
      super.onCreate(savedInstanceState)
      setContentView(R.layout.activity_main)

      mainViewModel =
ViewModelProvider(this).get(MainViewModel::class.java)

      mainViewModel.userName.observe(this, Observer { name ->
         findViewById<TextView>(R.id.textView).text = name
      })

      mainViewModel.fetchUserData()
```

```
  }
}
```

15.2.3 Room Database

Room is an abstraction layer over SQLite that provides a simple API to interact with databases. It reduces boilerplate code and is fully integrated with **LiveData** and **ViewModel**.

1. **Create the Entity:**

kotlin

```kotlin
@Entity(tableName = "users")
data class User(
    @PrimaryKey(autoGenerate = true) val id: Int,
    val name: String,
    val age: Int
)
```

2. **Create the DAO (Data Access Object):**

kotlin

```kotlin
@Dao
interface UserDao {
    @Insert
    suspend fun insert(user: User)

    @Query("SELECT * FROM users")
    fun getAllUsers(): LiveData<List<User>>
}
```

3. **Create the Database:**

kotlin

```kotlin
@Database(entities = [User::class], version = 1)
abstract class AppDatabase : RoomDatabase() {
    abstract fun userDao(): UserDao
}
```

4. **Using Room in ViewModel:**

kotlin

```kotlin
class UserViewModel(application: Application) :
AndroidViewModel(application) {
    private val userDao: UserDao =
AppDatabase.getDatabase(application).userDao()

    val allUsers: LiveData<List<User>> = userDao.getAllUsers()

    fun addUser(user: User) {
        viewModelScope.launch {
            userDao.insert(user)
        }
    }
}
```

By combining **Room, LiveData,** and **ViewModel,** you can create an architecture that supports data persistence and UI updates in a lifecycle-aware manner.

15.2.4 Using WorkManager for Background Tasks

WorkManager is ideal for scheduling background tasks that need to run reliably, even if the app is terminated or the device is rebooted. It supports tasks like syncing data, uploading files, and performing periodic operations.

Example of a one-time task using **WorkManager:**

kotlin

```kotlin
val workRequest = OneTimeWorkRequestBuilder<MyWorker>()
    .setInitialDelay(30, TimeUnit.MINUTES)
    .build()

WorkManager.getInstance(context).enqueue(workRequest)
```

This task will be executed even if the app is closed or the device is restarted, making **WorkManager** perfect for tasks like periodic data syncing.

15.3 Career Development in Android Development: Opportunities, Certifications, and Resources for Continued Learning

15.3.1 Career Opportunities in Android Development

The demand for Android developers continues to grow as more businesses develop mobile apps to engage customers. Android development offers a wide range of career opportunities, including roles in large enterprises, startups, freelance work, and even consulting. Below are a few career paths you can explore as an Android developer:

1. Junior Android Developer

Junior Android developers are typically responsible for building simple features, fixing bugs, and working under the guidance of senior developers. This is an entry-level position where you can learn and grow by working on various aspects of Android development.

2. Senior Android Developer

Senior Android developers have advanced skills and experience. They take the lead in designing and building complex features, mentoring junior developers, and ensuring that the app is scalable, maintainable, and performs well. A senior developer will often be responsible for code reviews, architecture decisions, and managing development timelines.

3. Android Architect

An Android architect is responsible for designing the overall architecture of large Android apps. They ensure that the app follows best practices and is scalable, modular, and maintainable. This role requires deep knowledge of Android architecture, design patterns, and advanced topics like performance optimization and security.

4. Mobile Development Lead / CTO

At the highest level, mobile development leads or Chief Technology Officers (CTOs) oversee the entire mobile development process, managing teams of developers and ensuring that mobile apps align with business goals. They typically have extensive experience in mobile technologies and leadership.

15.3.2 Android Development Certifications

Certifications are a great way to validate your skills and improve your resume. Below are some certifications you can pursue to advance your career as an Android developer:

1. Google Associate Android Developer Certification

The **Google Associate Android Developer Certification** is an entry-level certification that validates your ability to develop Android apps. It covers topics like user interface design, data management, and debugging, and is an excellent way to demonstrate your skills to potential employers.

2. Google Professional Android Developer Certification

This advanced certification is aimed at developers with experience in Android development. It tests your knowledge in areas like architecture, performance, security, and building production-level apps.

3. Coursera and Udacity Android Development Courses

Platforms like **Coursera** and **Udacity** offer Android development courses and certifications in partnership with Google. These programs offer hands-on learning and real-world projects that can help you improve your skills.

15.3.3 Continued Learning and Resources for Android Developers

As the Android ecosystem evolves, it's essential to keep learning and staying updated with the latest trends and tools. Here are some valuable resources for Android developers:

1. Official Android Documentation

The official Android documentation is the best place to start for in-depth information about Android APIs, libraries, and tools. The **Android Developer Guides** provide detailed tutorials, best practices, and code samples.

- Android Developer Documentation

2. Android Developers Blog

The **Android Developers Blog** is regularly updated with the latest news, features, and tips for Android developers. It provides valuable insights into new tools, frameworks, and practices in the Android ecosystem.

- Android Developers Blog

3. YouTube Channels and Online Tutorials

YouTube channels like **Android Developers** and **CodeWithHarry** offer tutorials, deep dives into new features, and other valuable content for developers.

4. GitHub Repositories

Explore open-source Android projects on **GitHub** to see real-world examples of how others are building Android apps. GitHub is an excellent resource for learning and contributing to the community.

- GitHub Android Repositories

Conclusion

Exploring advanced topics in Android development, including **Jetpack Libraries**, **Android Architecture Components**, and **career development opportunities**, is crucial for progressing in your Android development career. Jetpack libraries help you build modern, scalable, and maintainable apps, while Android Architecture Components empower you to implement robust app architectures. Continuing your learning journey through certifications, online resources, and hands-on practice will ensure that you remain up-to-date with the latest tools, technologies, and best practices in the Android ecosystem. By embracing these advanced topics and continuously improving your skills, you can take your Android development career to new heights and build apps that meet the demands of today's mobile-first world.

www.ingramcontent.com/pod-product-compliance
Lightning Source LLC
LaVergne TN
LVHW051335050326
832903LV00031B/3550